CONNECT AND GROW RICH

How To Earn a Fortune in Network Marketing

Natalia Dikun

Connect and Grow Rich. How to earn a Fortune in Network Marketing
Dikun, Natalia

Copyright © 2019 by Natalia Dikun

ISBN: 9781094773575

Disclaimer
No part of this publication may be reproduced, stored in a retrieval system, or transmitted in any form or by any means, electronic, mechanical, photocopying, recording, scanning or otherwise, without written permission from the copyright holder.

The advice contained in this material might not be suitable for everyone. The author obtained the information from sources believed to be reliable and from his own personal experience, but she neither implies nor intend any guarantee of accuracy.

All rights reserved, including the right to reproduce this book or portions thereof in any form whatsoever.

All characters are fictional, any coincidences are random.

The author and publisher never give legal, accounting, medical or any other type of professional advice. The reader must always seek those services from competent professionals that can review their own particular circumstances. The author and publisher particularly disclaim any liability, loss or risk taken by individuals who directly or indirectly act on the information contained herein. All readers must accept full responsibility for their use of this material.

Published by:
10-10-10 Publishing
Markham, Ontario

First 10-10-10 Publishing paperback edition April 2019

Contents

Dedication	vii
Foreword	ix
Acknowledgements	xi

Chapter 1: The Life of Your Dreams	**1**
My Story	1
The Life of Your Dreams	3
How to Become Financially Independent	5
Why is Network Marketing the Great Possibility of Creating Personal Well-being?	7
Network Marketing Myths	10
Everyone Can Do It	12

Chapter 2: How Can You Choose the Best Company?	**15**
Key Questions	15
Timing: How Long Has the Company Existed?	17
Company History and Philosophy	19
Products	21
What Should I Do To Make Money?	23
What Are the Work Systems?	25

Chapter 3: Make Your Decision — 27
The Golden Rule of Successful People — 27
Make a Decision — 28
Decision: No — 30
Yes, Maybe It's Interesting, but I Still Have Questions — 31
Decision: I Want to Become a Customer of the Company — 32
Decision: I Want to Become a Business Partner — 33

Chapter 4: The First Secrets of a Successful Start — 35
Nora's Story — 35
Find Your "Why" and Choose Your Goal — 37
Be 100% Sure — 40
Use the Products and Create Your Story — 42
How to React to "No" — 45

Chapter 5: What To Do Next — 49
Use, Love, and Explore Your Products — 49
Keep in Touch With the Sponsor — 50
Create a List of Contacts — 52
Qualify Your Contacts — 54
Invite, Invite, Invite — 56
How to Invite People — 57

Chapter 6: Several Ways To Do Business — 63
The First Appointments With Your Sponsor — 63
Launch Evening or Business Opening — 64
The Business Meeting — 66
Skype and Zoom Call — 68
One-to-One Presentation — 70
Webinar or Call — 72

Chapter 7: How To Be the Best in Follow-Up   75
Why Do You Need To Have Follow-Up?   75
When To Start Follow-Up   76
How To Get the Great Testimonials   78
Referrals: How To Get Them in Any Situation   79
How To Engage Customers in the Sales Process   81
How To Reward the Best Customers   82

Chapter 8: How To Reach the Next Level   85
Meet Markus   85
The Four Characteristics of Successful People   87
Take Massive Actions   89
Actions That Bring Earnings   90
Renew Your Commitment Regularly   92
The 90-Day Plan   94

Chapter 9: The Ultimate Secrets of Success   97
Our Business is the Business of People   97
How To Create Quality Contacts   98
Don't Abandon Your Base   100
Where To Find New Contacts   102
Attend Fairs and Events   103
Create Contacts Everywhere   105

Chapter 10: Connect and Grow Rich   107
Network Marketing is a Mentoring Activity   107
The Code of Honor   108
Promote and Participate in Your Company's Events   110
Follow the System or Create It   112
The Importance of Charity   113
Connect and Grow Rich   115

About the Author   119

I dedicate this book to my son, Alessandro, and my loving parents.

Foreword

Do you live the life of FREEDOM you want to have? Are you the author of your life? Do you want to be your own boss, travel the world, have more money and time for yourself and your family, but feel so frozen with fear because you do not know how to achieve this?

Would you like to discover your mission on this planet and fulfill it, getting richer, happier and healthier, and taking advantage of abundance and freedom?

Regardless of who you are or what your current situation is, regardless of your age, culture, profession and economic situation, *Connect and Grow Rich* will show you how to create additional and residual income in network marketing, how to choose the right company, and how to find your first customers and business partners.

Author Natalia Dikun was once an ordinary office employee, and a single mother who emigrated from Russia to Europe. Despite a good salary, she was worried about the financial future of her family. After a friend invited her to do network marketing, she began to work actively in this business, despite the fact that at first it was very difficult for her. Natalia is now Green Diamond, which is one of the highest and most prestigious ranks in the company with which she works. Natalia is a true example of what you can become, if you apply all that she teaches you in this book.

Natalia shares with you all her personal experiences to help you overcome fear and begin to build the kind of life you want to live. This guide will help you start a business in a network company that you choose, and will help you develop the skills you need to become an entrepreneur and manage your time and money.

Get ready to read this amazing journey and get ready for significant changes in your life, finances and live the LIFE OF YOUR DREAMS.

Raymond Aaron
New York Times Bestselling Author

Acknowledgements

Thanks ...

To my beloved parents, for raising me to be independent, creative, and purposeful.

To my son, Alessandro; he is the main reason for my determination to succeed, and he always believed in me and encouraged me. My caring family: my sister, niece, and my relatives, for their constant support and care. To my mentors and teachers: Helmut, for giving me this opportunity, and for teaching me the basics of this business and the laws of the Universe, as well as for his generosity; Birgit, for her example of hard work and perseverance; Chris, for teaching me an analytical approach to business; Manfred, for his great presentations from the stage; Stefan, for his optimism and dedication to the company; and to all my other mentors.

Thanks to all the people whose courses and classes I attended, and whose books that I read. Special thanks to all my team, friends, and colleagues for their hard work and the desire to achieve their goals and trust. Thanks to Stefano, Michele, Davide and Lucia, Paolo, Claudio, Antonio, and Maurizio and Elisabetta. Thanks to Daniela, for becoming my first business partner and believing in me. I warmly thank all the members of my team. Unfortunately, the size of this book does not allow me to thank you all by name, but I remember you, with gratitude. And of course, thanks to Raymond Aaron for believing in me and publishing my book.

1

The Life of Your Dreams

My Story

If someone had told me 6 years ago that I would live in London and start traveling around the world, talking from the stages, conducting training courses, advising people on business and writing books, I simply wouldn't have believed it. After all, this is now my life, and each of these wonderful changes started with a decision I made after talking to my friend, Emanuel—but let me tell you a little more.

My life has now changed drastically, but it all started 6 years ago.

During those years, I lived in Italy and worked in a company as a sales manager, but I was always looking for something that could improve my life, the life of my son, and my family.

I was born in Russia to a good family. My mother was a teacher, and my father was an artist; he was the director of a youth theater. He was writing poetry and songs, so my sister and I studied at a music school. At the end of my studies at the high school, I started teaching music to children. A few years later, I moved to St. Petersburg where, after completing my university studies, I became a tourism manager.

I wanted to discover Europe; therefore, I had settled in northern Italy, where I worked in the tourism sector.

I then became manager of a company that works with Eastern Europe; but at that time, everything else in my life was difficult. I separated from my husband and found myself raising my son alone. My mom helped me, and I am and always will be very grateful, but it was still very difficult for me. The situation and financial stability of myself and my family worried me. Everything was influenced by the situation in which I was living, and I had too little time to be with my son. I had to constantly go to numerous fairs and visit clients, and I was often traveling. I was very tired and constantly worried. If I had not gone to work for any reason, my family would have been short of livelihood in a short time. I dreamed of traveling for pleasure. I also wanted my son to study in the most prestigious universities, and I wanted to help my family.

When my good friend, Emanuel, called me one day, telling me he wanted to talk to me about a possibility that would improve my life, I immediately became curious. He told me he would tell me about a new company that sold health products. I have always been interested in the health and care of myself, so I always try to be as presentable as possible.

I liked his proposal and decided to try the products. He told me that if I liked the products, I could also make money through them. Initially, I was very skeptical because I had already been offered something similar once, but I hadn't earned anything; but this time I decided to accept and start anyway. I really liked the products. They made me feel good.

The phrase that my friend had said about the fact that I could earn on the products, and even become a financially free person, came back to me constantly, without giving me peace. And then I decided to ask him what he had in mind.

Emanuel replied that it was a long story, and he invited me to pay him a visit.

The Life of Your Dreams

I sat with Emanuel, around the table in his garden, and the sun warmed us gently. We started to talk, and he started asking me several questions:

"How would you like your life to be? Where would you live? With whom? Would you like to live in the city? In the country side? By the sea? In an exotic country? What would you like to do? If you had all the money and all the time, what would you do? What would your day be like? What time would you wake up? What would you do next? What would you eat for breakfast? Who would you do it with? What would your car be like? Or would you like to fly a helicopter? "

I started laughing.

"A helicopter?!" I said in amazement.

"What would you do during the day? Would you read a book? Would you eat with friends, with your family? What would your days be like? Where would you go on vacation?" he continued to ask.

I never wondered before how I imagined my ideal life.

I asked Emanuel, "Why are you asking me all these questions?"

He replied, "Because if you don't know where to go, how do you get there?"

It's true! I thought. I paused to think about it. I looked around and saw Emanuel's beautiful house, and thought that he probably lived the life of his dreams. He was very serene, he was in no hurry, and he had no stress. There were few people I had seen so serene in my life. Emanuel explained to me that before going somewhere, you have to have a goal. It's like going on vacation. First we decide where we want to go. Then we start looking for a hotel or a home. Then we choose the means of transport, and we start planning our journey to get everything ready and know everything before arriving. It was precisely for this reason that Emanuel asked me to describe how I wanted my life.

He told me, "When you go home, take a nice notebook and start writing down all your dreams. Write the answers to the questions I asked you, but don't think too much; write the first thing that comes to mind. Also, write how much you would like to earn per month and year. How would you like your family to be, and where would you like to go on vacation? What kind of relationships do you have with your loved ones? Write for several days. When you see that some things will be repeated day after day, it will mean that those will be your true desires. Focus on your potential and on everything that gives value to your person, and you will see that, in this way, you can design the life of your dreams."

Then I interrupted him, and with mild disappointment and a tone of protest, I said, "I work hard all day, but I barely manage to pay all the bills and set aside some money for my son's studies. How do I get to have the life of my dreams?"

"We will talk about this next time, dear Natalia," he replied, leaving me in suspense.

When I speak on the stage during my courses, or when I do a coaching section for someone, I like to ask people this question: "How do you see your ideal life?" It is important to see the goal. For this reason, dear friends, I ask you to leave the book now, take half an hour, and write how you imagine the life of your dreams.

On my website, you will find a document that you can download to help you better design the life of your dreams.

Take a notebook right away, set the timer on your watch for 30 minutes, and start describing the life of your dreams.

How to Become Financially Independent

I returned to Emanuel after a few days, and I had a notebook with me, full of notes. During those days, I wrote down all my dreams, and the ideas that were in my mind, as I wanted my life to be. I described my ideal home and my future family, and I also described the university where I dreamed my son would study. I described the car I wanted, and how I would spend the time. I wrote that I wanted to travel and visit distant countries like Thailand, Maldives, Philippines, America, and a thousand others...

I began to see my future and my ideal life clearer, but together with all this, I started to have even more questions and concerns. I asked Emanuel, "But how do I get the life of my dreams? Although I work so hard and live an absolutely normal life, I can't call it the life of my dreams. If I didn't work, I wouldn't even be able to pay the bills, and in that case, it certainly wouldn't be the wonderful and comfortable life that I would like. What should I do?"

"You did your homework well, and you also asked good questions," said Emanuel. "I like people who ask the questions," he added. "Do you know what the difference is between an economically poor person and a wealthy person?" he asked me.

"Of course; the poor person does not have the money, and the wealthy person does."

"Yes, that's partly true, but the biggest difference is in the way they face the world and see the gains. The poor or average person works for the gain: they go to work and are paid by the hour. Or, in the case of professionals, such as doctors, architects or lawyers, they are paid for the results. But although these people make good money, if they didn't go to work every day, they wouldn't earn anything, right?"

"Yes, that's right," I agreed.

"And what do wealthy, rich people do?" asked Emanuel. "They work for the revenue or residual income. They make sure they still make money while not going to work."

"It would be really nice," I exclaimed. "But how do they do it?"

"There are so many ways to create the residual income. For example, you can inherit a large sum of money from a relative, invest this money in the bank, and live on the interest," he explained.

"But I don't have rich relatives," I said with disappointment.

"I didn't have any either," smiled Emanuel. "And there are very few people in this world who can become wealthy like this. You could even marry a rich person."

I shook my head. "The rich people I know are already married."

"You could write a song or a book that would become a

best seller, and you could live off royalties," he suggested.

"It's true!" I exclaimed. "I studied music, but it's hard for me to be able to write a hit. You could also buy real estate, rent it, and live on the income," I suggested. "But I need a big capital, and I don't have it," I replied.

"This is a problem in every way, for the average normal person, and there is no possibility of creating an income or a passive gain, except one ...," Emanuel began in a mysterious way and then paused.

"What is this way?" I asked. "Tell me," I insisted.

"It's called *network marketing*."

Why is Network Marketing the Great Possibility of Creating Personal Well-being?

"Why are you so sure?"

"Because I know it," said Emanuel. "Because I started and knew network marketing many years ago. I am a very simple person. I was a simple clerk, while now, I live in my villa, and I earn a lot of money. I have helped many people. I have traveled much of the world, and my children study abroad. I have a good life, and now I can say that I have a residual gain. And I can explain this to you, because everyone can change their life for the better, by knowing network marketing and starting to work in this industry. First of all, the products of network marketing, or the services offered by a company, are very effective. Usually, no sales experience is required to become a business partner," he concluded.

"And how does a person have success if the products are not good?"

"For this, a person must start using the products, and

love them, and then learn this activity. Another reason why network marketing is a unique opportunity is because it is within everyone's reach. Everyone can afford to start a business like this. Usually, all companies allow a person with a few hundred euros, dollars, or pounds to start their own business. Let's look at the traditional business world. For example, do you want to open a bar? How much does it cost you to open it? You need a license. You need to find a space. Do the works. Buy the equipment. How much does it cost you? Surely, you've already exceeded 10 thousand euros, pounds, or dollars. Also, add the costs of products like coffee, confectionery, and all the other things you sell. Add the cost of the staff, and add the cost of advertising. It means that to start a small business, you need considerable capital. In network marketing, you can start from 50, 100, 200, and up to € 1000 or £ in start-up costs.

"The third and very important thing is that your activity in network marketing is only to share information on products or opportunity. The company will take care of personnel, logistics, customer relations, the opening of new offices and markets, the production of goods, and also warehousing. This means that you need to learn a few skills, and in these, to become a master.

"Another very important thing is that you can start your business simply during the free hours of the day or the week. You don't have to leave your current job or business. You don't have to upset your life. Through network marketing, you can earn extra money, create a small income, and you can really build an empire. I'll give you an example. Even if you have little time and a full-time job, do you have some time to devote to your future?" Emanuel asked me.

"Yes, of course," I replied.

"Well, how much time do you have?" he continued.

"An hour a day," I said.

"Okay. Suppose you start working with a company for an hour a day. You use the products, and you find the first customers and the first collaborators. Even your business partners will probably have little time to devote to the new business—maybe just an hour a day. However, when you work alone, you do 6 hours a week. When you have two collaborators, your time is duplicated, and you have 18 hours a week: 6 of yours, plus 6 of the two collaborators. Imagine if they began to invite other people too. Your time would begin to multiply. Even if not all of them are very active, there would be more and more people who would still add their time and efforts, creating their own profit and also benefiting you.

"Our time is limited; however, through your collaborators, you multiply the hours and the results. In a few months, if you are more active, or even if you continue to work an hour a day, the result will be twenty, a hundred, or a thousand hours a week. This is the secret of wealthy people, and this is the secret of the passive income that everyone would like to have," concluded Emanuel.

This speech completely fascinated me. Dear Reader, just imagine! A simple person like you can start from scratch, but with so many other people, you can create a residual income, like the richest people on the planet Earth do. This is really great!

Network Marketing Myths

"There are many myths about network marketing that I want to reveal to you," said Emanuel. "The first is that you have to be a good salesman. The most important thing is that the person loves the product or service that his company offers. During these years, I met many people who were excellent salesmen, but they didn't last long. Who really wins is not the one who sells more but the one who involves more people to use and share products and opportunity. Indeed, being too good at selling sometimes does not help because, if you have a business partner in your team that is not as good as you are in sales, he or she may think that the business is only for salespeople. If a person bases his activity only on sales in network marketing, but does not devote the time to build a network of collaborators, and to train them and make them strong and independent, his career can end very soon. When a seller is tired of selling, he produces nothing, he gains nothing, and he becomes demotivated, and at this point, he gives up.

"If, instead, a person uses the product or service, gets a great result, learns to present it effectively, manages to sell the product without being the professional seller, and can find new business partners, this begins to create an indirect or residual income. Even if this person does not sell for a few days, he does not go into crisis because he still receives earnings and is motivated," said Emanuel.

"Another very common myth is that to achieve success in network marketing, it is enough to invite two or three people. It is a wrong concept. Some companies allow you to make a career having two or three strong teams;

however, these two or three may not happen right away. When someone arrives, telling you that you have to invite only two people, be alert, because this person is not telling you the truth," he informed me.

"It may be that you find champions in the sector fast enough. However, it may also happen that we need more time and effort. Many people believed these false promises about inviting few people, and immediately becoming millionaires, but then they were very disappointed. I propose that you see this process as a children's coach does," Emanuel suggested.

"A coach, when working with children, can say that a child has more potential, or that another has more character, but no one can which of them will be the true champion who could one day win the Olympics. So, only by inviting so many people will you find your champions, so that together, you will go to victory. Inviting is not a difficult job, and if you know this myth, you will not fall into a trap."

I remembered a friend's story about when someone suggested her, and she became part of some company. The person who enrolled her assured her that she would only have to find two people. I remember that he talked to a dozen people, including me, but none of them did much, and his enthusiasm vanished. This is exactly what Manuel spoke of.

"Another myth about network marketing is based on the idea that companies pay if people become part of network marketing. This is not legal. For this reason, if someone were to propose you a network marketing activity where you earn because other people pay to enter, and there are no goods, products, or services behind it, stay away from this proposal. If you want to build a solid and lasting future in network marketing, you must choose a good foundation. At the base, there must be an excellent product that will give results, but we'll talk better than this another time," he said, and then continued:

"Another very popular myth is that you have to have a lot of time, and that you have to quit your job. As I explained to you before, you only need one hour a day, or a few hours a week. If you work consistently and methodically, using a system, you can achieve excellent results. It is only when your earnings in network marketing begin to exceed the earnings of the main job constantly, for at least 6 months, that you can consider the idea of leaving your job if you don't like it. For this reason, the idea that you need a lot of time, or that you have to leave your job to work in network marketing, is a myth," he concluded.

When I went away from Emanuel, I said to myself, *"I have decided to find my champions! I will invite as many people as needed. And I will find my champions among them."*

Everyone Can Do It

"In reality," Emanuel said, "we are doing network marketing all the time. When we go to a good restaurant, or when we read a good book or have seen a good movie, we share our enthusiasm and knowledge with friends. But we are not paid for this. Some companies that work in telephony, use this principle. Do you remember: 'If you bring a friend, you will have € 10 discount on the next bill?' The gyms also use it now: 'If you bring a friend, you have a free month's subscription.' The idea is beautiful—only the company does not pay us; it gives us extra little gifts. Furthermore, once this friend has been brought, the company has earned a customer, and extra money, while we have earned nothing concrete.

"This is not the case in network marketing. When you register as an affiliate of a company, you receive a personal code. Every time you talk to someone, share your experience and your story, and your friend becomes a customer or an affiliate, the company rewards you. And it does not end here; you are rewarded even when the thing is duplicated, and when your friend brings other friends, who in turn become customers or business partners of the company. It's word of mouth that rewards you. This is why network marketing is a natural thing, which we normally do every day, without being a salesman and without much effort."

2

How Do You Choose the Best Company?

Key Questions

I stared at Emanuel, and I asked him, "How can you know if a company is the right one for you?"

"That's a good question," he said, introducing the real answer. "It's a good question because it is an important choice. It is like when you make choices in life: if you make the right choice, you will see positive consequences; but if you make bad decisions, it will be the opposite. For example, when you were a teen and you had to look for the right boy to be your boyfriend, it might be that you were hanging out with a boy that made you laugh and have fun, but the family life didn't suit him that much. So, even if at the time you thought that he was the right one, thinking to the future, your eventual marriage wouldn't be that happy. On the other hand, if you had another guy whose lifestyle and mind were different, and he was responsible, kind, and trustful, and you liked him too, there would be more of a chance for a happy marriage.

"When you are going to choose a company, try to use some standards, just as you would have done when you were a teen. In the case of a company, your checks could be: where does it come from; what is the story behind it; how long has it existed, and in how many countries? The world has become smaller and faster. For that reason, it would be better to not just work nationally but also in an international way. Thanks to the internet, we have this big chance. Also, another important aspect are the products or services that a company offers. Is it a current product? Is it useful? Is it in trend? I'll tell you about a trend product later," he said, taking a break before he started to talk again.

"Through the story of the company and one of the founders, you have to understand if the company has a philosophy, because if it doesn't have one, that means that they don't want to make a long-term business. Are you interested in doing a business right for a couple of years, or would you like the results of your business to help your children and your children's children in the future?" he asked.

"Of course, I'd like to do one in the long run," I said.

"Perfect," said Emanuel. "Many times, at the beginning, you don't understand how much you have to do to make money in a company. If you have to make too many sales, you have to realise that you have to have a lot of time to be a good seller, but how many people can be considered good salesmen, and how many people love selling?

It's not that hard to see, but we must pay attention to these things as well, and we must pay attention to the working methods that you cannot use," my mentor warned me.

"Does the company offer me the tools that facilitate the business, or should I use the 'door-to-door' method? Because if that's the case, I have to waste too much time going to visit the customers, and I have to find so many, so I might let it go," I said.

"Now, I'll explain in more detail what questions you need to ask when someone offers you a network marketing activity, and if the answer to these questions is positive, then you can consider this company as a good partner for a lasting and successful business for you and for your family. Remember Natalia, once you find the right partner, it's up to you to start working, and to create your future, because it's like a marriage: even if you found the right partner, you have to make the effort, spend time, and make a commitment to have a happy family life. But let me better explain to you how you can find the right company for you," he said.

Timing: How Long Has the Company Existed?

"This question is very important," said Emanuel. "Try to ask the person who introduced you to the activity. If you've already been told in the presentation, pay attention to this fact. Now I'll explain why.

"As we know, all companies go through three phases. In the first phase, the company establishes itself, and nobody notices that it exists on the market. In this phase, the company is ignored. This phase can last up to three years. In the second phase, the company is known, and if it has made good progress, it is also fought by competitors. This phase lasts about two or three years. During the third phase, the company is recognised and respected. This is the right phase to start working with the company. I'll explain: Statistics say that more than 92% of companies close during the first five years of activity. It is understandable why, if in the first phase, the company must settle down, and in the second phase, everything is even more difficult because it is fought. Therefore, only after 5–6 years of activity can the company prove itself to be able to be on the market. Now, think of yourself as a new collaborator: At what stage in the life of the company is it better to enter? Some people think it is at the beginning. When someone comes to you and says, 'Wow! We are the first on the market! The company opened just a year or two ago. Come with me, and we'll make big money!'

"But where is the security that the company will survive and manage to overcome the first 2–3 years of its life? And if it fails a little later? It means that you have wasted a year or two of your life, you have questioned your reputation, and maybe you have made a bad impression with your friends and family. Unfortunately, I have already seen many companies in these years," said Emanuel. "They came and left, like a comet."

"The real question is: Are you ready to risk your time, your energy, and your reputation, or would you look more closely at other similar proposals?" he asked.

"I'd be much more careful," I replied.

"In the second phase," continued Emanuel, "in my opinion, it is even more risky to enter. If the company is fought by competitors and mass media, then it will be difficult for you to achieve success, because the time for the company is wrong. It is very difficult to change people's opinions today, especially since it is dictated by the mass media. For this reason, I invite you to pay attention if the company you are proposing is at this stage.Everything changes when the company is already approved, when it has received awards, and when it is part of a supervisory body, such as DSA (Direct Salling Association), Seldia, Avedisco, or other quality control associations for companies in the sector. At this stage, I advise you to enter!

"If the company has survived in the first 5–6 years of its activity, it has already proven that it is based on sound principles, the product is required, and the compensation plan is right. This means that the company has a good reputation, and perhaps it has also received some awards, which also helps you. Starting with a company at the right time is always a part of success. For this reason, when they tell you the story of the company, listen to it well: When was it founded; how long has it existed? This guarantees you don't make mistakes and don't take too many risks.

"Another very important thing is the timing. Few people know this phenomenon. The timing tells you what stage the company is in, in your country. If the company has existed for more than 10 or 15 years in your country, the market is likely to be quite saturated. If instead, the company has passed the first 5–6 years, or even 10 years, but in your country it is in the first 5–6 years, then this is the ideal phase, because the company is new and dynamic. It's new, and people love news. Those who start at this stage are very likely to achieve economic independence.

"Remember well," added Emanuel. "These two questions must be clear during the presentation: How long has the company existed, and what is the timing?" he concluded.

Company History and Philosophy

"The second question you have to ask, when someone makes you a proposal to work with a network marketing company, is who the founders are, and what the history and philosophy of the company are. Why is it so important?

"I'll give you an example of family life. When you choose a man for a relationship, you like him, and things get pretty serious. Surely, you want to know what kind of family he comes from. Get to know his parents, where they live, and how they behave. Talk to them, and understand if the background of this man or this family could give you some nasty surprises or nice surprises. So, when choosing a company, pay attention, and ask more questions when they tell you about the founders, their history, and their backgrounds. If it is a company created by a group of people who do not have a good background in the sector, in business or in general, and if during the presentation, there are not enough facts about the founders, do your research. Look carefully at the reputation of the founders, or if it is only a group of people who have decided to make some money. Often, it's just money for themselves. Remember that choosing a company in network marketing is like choosing a partner in traditional business, or a partner in life. For this reason, take some time and try to find out more about the founders and the company's philosophy.

"There is nothing wrong with earning money, but if the company does not have a healthy philosophy (for example, helping people get better or healthier), it could be that the company won't last long. There are these projects created specifically to make fast money, especially in the digital world; however, the practice teaches that very few of these companies lasted more than two or three years. Why do you want to join a company? Perhaps because you like the product, but if you enter as a business partner, it is certainly because of your desire to earn money and create a passive income. But a passive income is only possible when the project is long-term. If the project lasts and pays for only two years, it does not create a residual profit but only a quick profit.

"Regarding the company's philosophy, another thing that could give you a good sign is the presence of a charity fund. It is one of the universal laws: You must give back to the world if you have received something good. For this reason, if a company has a charity fund, it's a good sign," concluded Emanuel.

Products

"Usually, a network marketing company offers very effective products or services, because they must be sold by non-professional people. It is always better to check the quality and effectiveness of the products by using them personally. When I train people who want to be successful in network marketing, I always stress the importance of using products regularly."

Returning to Emanuel's house, he continued: "To succeed in the long term, you must ask yourself: What are the products and services that the company offers? Is it a trend product? It can be a good product, but if it is no longer trendy and is no longer current, it is not a good idea for you to do business."

"I'll give you an example," said Emanuel. "Have you ever seen a videotape?" he asked.

"Yes, I still have some at my house," I replied.

"Do you use them?" he asked.

"No," I said.

"You see, some fifteen years ago, videotapes were a real cult. Everybody opened videotape rental points, and there were lines to go and take video tapes, while now you don't even see one anymore. For this reason, the product must be a trend, and it must be current. What is a trend? A trend is something popular and in demand. It could be all that concerns the human being, and everything that can help people to be more effective, to feel better, and to present themselves better. This will surely be a TREND for the next twenty years. It must also be a consumer product, because if a product is a trend but is not a product that is consumed and snapped up, for you as a business partner, it is not good business," explained Emanuel.

"Why?" I asked.

"Because you will always have to find new customers. For example, if you sell a machine that the person can use for 2, 3, or 5 years, you earn when you sell, but later on, you will be forced to look for another customer. With the consumer product, it is different. Once you acquire a customer and get good follow-up, you won't have to worry too much, because people require this product for months and sometimes for years. Therefore, many companies, selling equipment, sell additional goods to them (so-called back-sales) so that customers continue to order. This is the basis of the passive income.

"Another parameter is the number of products offered by the company because, if there are many, it will be very difficult to learn and try them all. It will also be difficult to offer them to a person because we all have little time today. People have little time to listen to us, and cannot memorise so much information, because we are bombarded with lots of information. When the company offers few and effective products or services, you have a winning company for doing business."

"It's true," I said. "When you told me that the company has only a few products, you immediately intrigued me, because I had neither the desire nor the time to study too much," I revealed.

"From personal experience, it is better to choose a company that proposes trend and consumer products," stated Emanuel.

What Should I Do To Make Money?

"When they present you a marketing company," said Emanuel, "you have to pay close attention to how you earn. It is not easy for a person, who has no experience in network marketing, to understand the answers.

"Does everyone say, during the presentation, that their company is better? But is it really so? Check it out! Ask them when you will start earning. If the answer is 'immediately,' it is a good answer. Check that you will only earn when you move a product or service on the market. Do not fall into the trap of some companies that do not offer this, and attract people by telling them that they will only earn by inviting people who bring money through registration. These schemes are illegal, and you will not want to do anything that is not legal, right?"

"Sure," I replied.

"Perfect! If you earn immediately by selling the products, or finding a collaborator who purchases the products for personal use or for sale, it is completely legal. Also, ask what you need to do to keep your earnings. I worked years ago for a company that had excellent products, but to earn my monthly allowance, I had to buy the products and possibly sell them for several thousand euros a month. Although I loved these products, having the products in such large quantities, at home, every year, I was tired of it. They clogged my garage, and I felt exhausted by continuing to sell products in large quantities.

"This does not correspond to the idea of creating passive income, because it becomes a sales activity, and today, we have too little time and many products on the market to dedicate ourselves only to sales. Ask the person, who presents the project to you, how many you will have to sell (or what personal turnover you should produce) in a month to keep your earnings from the network. If it's an achievable figure, then it's a good company for you. But if on the way, you have to buy more and more products to receive your earnings, you will have to make too much effort to be able to earn, and you will probably not be able to earn at all.

"At this point, you also ask how many people are earning. Let me give you an example: Ask if the person who is presenting the business to you is a successful person, and if he is not, let him introduce a successful person with whom you can possibly work. It is also important to have a good mentor in our business. If the answers you've received are positive, then that is great! You have found the company with which you can truly create your future."

"But there is still one last question to check," he added, leaving me in suspense.

How Do You Choose the Best Company?

What Are the Work Systems?

"Ask the person who proposes the activity to you, what the work systems are that the company uses. We are all very busy nowadays; the pace of life is hectic. In the 80s and 90s, when I started, it was very fashionable to call people and have a party at home, or invite them to a meeting at a hotel. Today, it is more difficult: We all have little time; we have a lot of work; and we have to share our time between work, family, and social commitments. On the other hand, however, we have the Internet, which, at times, we do not use effectively, but when we can, we can learn how to do business with it.

"Find out if the company has tools that allow you to work with so many people via the Internet, or if you simply work in traditional ways, using methods such as door-to-door. However, this also depends on you. If you are a person who does not like technology, it could also be good for you if the company does not offer technological support. However, remember that the majority of our future customers use the Internet and love technology. For this reason, check if the company you're interested in has systems to create an income. These tools must also be simple to use. Everything must be simple and duplicable. The strong point of network marketing is to learn a few simple steps and teach them to other people so that they, too, can teach them to others. This is called duplication, and it is the real key to creating residual income in network marketing. Now, dear Natalia, you have all the questions you need, to find the answers to decide whether it is the company, or not, to create your future in network marketing. Search for the answers to all these questions, and take the next step," concluded my mentor.

3

Make Your Decision

The Golden Rule of Successful People

We were sitting in Emanuel's luxurious living room, and we were talking about success. I asked: "What is the number one secret of successful people?"

He reflected for a moment and then replied: "The golden rule of successful people is to do things within 72 hours."

"Can you explain yourself better?" I asked.

"Yes, of course," he replied.

"When you have received information, it is never by chance. This information came to you for a reason. You must reflect, and you must evaluate this information as an opportunity, and within 72 hours, you have to decide what you want to do with this opportunity. Successful people do it, and that's why they get amazing results. Sometimes they make a wrong decision; it doesn't matter. But since they have, nevertheless, begun to act, actions always lead to results. In life, those who have achieved great success are not those who have always made the right decisions; they are those who have done more actions and made more decisions. Instead, ordinary people tend to procrastinate.

They do not want to decide, and they do not realize that when these 72 hours have passed, in which you still have all the very clear information, that was the best time to make a decision and take action. I don't know if you've ever attended a training course."

"Yes," I answered.

"Do you remember? You were so enthusiastic, and you wanted to change your life radically! The course lasted Saturday and Sunday, and then on Monday, you went to work; you had little time! The next day was the same. The information you have learned in this course remains as theories, if you do not start with new actions within 72 hours. You realize that after a month, your life is always the same, and you haven't made any changes, even if the intentions were excellent. The same thing happens when, at the beginning of a new year, we make good intentions (for example, starting to do gymnastics, or running every morning, or at least three times a week). If we don't start doing it immediately, within 72 hours, we definitely start procrastinating, and maybe we don't start doing gymnastics at all. In network marketing, as in any business, this golden rule always applies. This is why, when you have a presentation, you ask the questions I taught you, analyze the answers, make your decision within 72 hours, and take action!"

Make a Decision

Emanuel continued to teach me:

"In life, it is very important to learn how to make decisions; even if we often try to avoid it, having this habit is necessary. As a wise person once said, 'It is better to

Make Your Decision

make a wrong decision than not to decide at all.' After all, if we don't make a decision, someone else will make it for us. And it is still not certain if we will appreciate the consequences that we will later receive for the choice of someone else.

"When you have known the company and its products, and have evaluated according to the criteria I described at the beginning, you can understand whether this company is right for you or not. And if it is, how do you want to participate? You can try the products and see how much you like them, or use the service of the company, if it's services and not products. In short, you can become a customer of the company. Above all, make your decision. Or, you become a business partner.

"The rule that all successful people follow is: Do an action within 72 hours! We talked about this before. That is, make a decision; if not immediately, at least within the first 72 hours!"

Soon, I will explain to you what decisions you can make, but for now, let's do some practice. Take a piece of paper and write 3 decisions of things to do today, in the next three days, and the following week. Write it down!

For example: I decided to go to bed today before midnight;

I decided to find and call (write) my ten schoolmates, in the next 3 days;

I decided not to eat after 7:00 pm for the whole week. I'll start today!

This exercise develops the habit of making decisions.

Take 5 minutes and do this exercise. And then go to the next chapter.

Decision: No

"There are four types of decisions. Now I will start from the first—more negative, but only at first sight. Richard Branson once said, in his book, to always say yes to opportunities. This is really another rule for successful people. But unfortunately, many of the people are not successful; not because we lack the talents or because we are lazy, but simply because we have been mistakenly raised. No one has taken care to make us grow as successful people. So many people don't even think about it at all. From our childhood, decisions are made for us: initially by parents, then educators and teachers, then friends, spouses, or employers. Therefore, very few people have the courage and the habit of making an independent decision. And even when they take it, they tend to say no to new things, and give up the possibility of changing their lives for the better. But this is another story.

"So, when a person has listened to the presentation and says no, we must certainly respect his decision. In general, the person said no—not to the company, or to us who represent it, but to himself, and to his chances of change. Of course, if you understand from the information received that the conditions we talked about before are not met, then it is fair to say no.

"If you already see that the company does not intend to do long-term business, or if you are not sure of the quality of the products, or you have doubts about the compensation plan or another aspect of the company, then say no! It is your right, and no one is allowed to persuade you. In this case, to say *no* would be the wise decision. If instead, you answered yes to all the questions above, then why do you say no? Just because you're so used to it? Why are you afraid of changes?

"Remember when we were told in childhood: Do not touch this; do not take that; you can't do it; do not talk to strangers; and so on? Therefore, we were educated in the habit of saying no, and to say *no* to the stimulating and positive possibilities for us.

"So, if you asked the right questions we talked about in the previous chapter, and received a positive answer to all these questions, think carefully! Don't give up the opportunity out of habit. Network marketing is a unique opportunity for ordinary people to achieve financial independence. Therefore, even if you said NO to the company that you don't think is right for you, keep looking for your opportunity," concluded Emanuel.

"Yes!" I exclaimed. "Those who seek will always find!"

Yes, Maybe It's Interesting, but I Still Have Questions

"Of course, when you have questions, it's okay, because it means you thought about it and decided to analyze everything carefully. The only problem is that sometimes this attitude becomes just an excuse for not making a final decision. But you remember, always: It is better to make the wrong decision than not to make it at all because, when you don't make a decision, someone else will make it for you," Emanuel replied to me.

"This could happen with your spouse, your boss, your friends, or relatives. And then, don't forget to ask yourself how much you might really like the consequences of a decision someone else has made for you. Remember, never give someone else the responsibility of your life and your choices. Take responsibility for everything that happens in your life.

"If you still have specific questions, choose three of the most important ones. Tell the person who gave you the presentation: 'If you answer these questions, I will be ready to make a decision.' If the person responds, and you are satisfied, everything is fine, but if he cannot answer, ask to meet his sponsor or his mentor (successful up line). Make sure you find someone who can answer these important questions for you, and ask them for the final answers once they are obtained, and then make a decision: either yes or no," he concluded.

Decision: I Want to Become a Customer of the Company

Emanuel began to speak:
"Decision: 'Yes, I liked the company, but I'm not ready to become a business partner. I want to try the products as a customer.' This is a good solution! First, because you give the opportunity a chance! Remember the rule of successful people: 'Always say yes to the opportunity.'

"Secondly, this is a good decision because most of the success of network marketing depends on the product. If the product is good and has helped you, you will love it so much that you can recommend it with conviction, love, and confidence, which will help other people, and you will have many chances to become a successful business partner in the future.

"Third, by doing this regularly, enough times and with the right beliefs, you will succeed. Furthermore, the knowledge of the product, and the love for it, is the first condition—and the most important condition—for success in network marketing," he concluded, and then continued shortly after.

"For many years of my career, I've seen people become customers and achieve excellent results using the company's products. Then, their friends started asking them how they managed to get such wonderful changes, and so they became their customers or business partners. They have learned to do this job professionally, and the growing activity has become an income. But the most important thing is that, at the beginning, they decided to try the product and took it seriously. This is, therefore, a very wise decision. You will get the result from the product, solve the problem, and in the future, you will have all the possibilities of success as a business partner," concluded my mentor.

Decision: I Want to Become a Business Partner

"And finally, here is the last decision: to become a business partner that, personally, I believe to be the best!" exclaimed Emanuel. "Why do I consider it the best? Because you give yourself the chance to build a completely new and wonderful life. You give yourself the opportunity to start earning extra money and, thus, to build a passive income. You give yourself the opportunity to meet new people, acquire new skills, travel to new places, and work with other people—with those you like," he said.

"Oh! This is very, very interesting!" I exclaimed.

"But above all," Emanuel continued, "You give yourself the opportunity to achieve financial independence, which is very important! As you will remember, only 3% of the world's population, at age 60, is financially independent and free. The remaining 97% needs the support of relatives or the state. So, by becoming a partner of the right company, you give yourself the opportunity to enter this elite circle.

"You will have time and money to do what you really love, and not to earn money to pay bills, day after day, year after year. Of course, this is just the beginning, and you will have to learn a lot, but the main thing is that you have made such a decision," concluded Emanuel.

I took this decree six years ago, and I never regret it. If you too, dear reader, make such a decision, read the book further, and you will see that it will help you learn the basic principles and skills necessary for success in network marketing. And then you will have to train and learn more, and you will reach new victories!

If you've read the book up to this point, you already know why network marketing is such a unique opportunity for any ordinary person to achieve financial independence and make their life more satisfying and happy. After all, we help other people, and that brings happiness.

If you still have doubts, or have decided to become a customer of the company, read on; you will have more information and clarity.

I thanked Emanuel for his excellent explanation, and for his time, and started my career as a business partner of the company.

My journey into the world of success had begun, but we will talk more about it in the next chapter.

4

The First Secrets of a Successful Start

Nora's Story

I decided to become a business partner and, as Emanuel advised, I took the products and got a wonderful result. I had my friends and acquaintances try them, and I invited them to start a business with me. Some started with me, but I wasn't very happy with the results. I expected more.

I wanted to change my life for the better; so much so that I started looking for a person who would teach me to do business faster and more efficiently. At an event, I saw our European leader. She was a woman named Nora, and she lived in Switzerland. This woman had made an amazing career and earned a lot of money.

I followed her throughout the event and asked her many questions. I wrote down everything she told me. The following week, I gave presentations like she did, and I used her method to attract people's attention. I did everything just as she advised me. I immediately started to make progress, but this was not enough for me. So, I decided to go to Nora and talk to her. I called her and asked her if I could spend a few days with her to learn how to start our business successfully. She was probably surprised that I wanted to go to her. But apparently, having heard in my voice such a desire to achieve success, she accepted.

I booked a hotel, took my car, and went to Switzerland. It was a fantastic journey: the majestic mountains, the magnificent landscapes outside the window—everything around me contributed to making everything wonderful. I saw a huge lake, so I stopped and admired the splendid view, and enjoyed the moment. Soon, I arrived at the villa where Nora lived with her husband. I was very excited. I rang the bell of the cast iron gate. The door opened, and I drove my car toward the wonderful courtyard. They greeted me cordially; we drank coffee and sat in the large living room to talk. The living room was furnished with great taste: elegant soft sofas made of white leather, antique rugs, and Chinese vases. But the most surprising thing was Nora's work table, with a huge screen and a magnificent view of the lake.

I smiled, and with a slight sigh, I said, "It will be a pleasure to work in this atmosphere." Nora returned the smile.

"Honey, you also have the opportunity to earn lots of money and live in a nice house. After all, you will understand that this has not always been the case. I, too, started many years ago as a newbie in this business. I was an employee of a state institution. A friend of mine invited me to go to a meeting one evening, and I took part in it for the company. I saw an old woman on stage saying she had made a lot of money, but I didn't think it could really be that way. And when the event host asked us, 'Who among you wants to earn $1,000,000?' I saw that several people had raised their hands. I, however, being shy, didn't do it."

The First Secrets of a Successful Start

"Which one of you wants to live in a beautiful villa?" he continued.

Then, I timidly raised my hand.

For some reason, he came to me and asked me, "Do you think you will live in a beautiful villa?"

"No," I replied in a low voice.

He sighed and said, "Don't worry. If you don't believe it, then you won't live there!"

"I looked at him with round eyes," said Norah, and this phrase attracted me.

"I couldn't understand how that simple old lady earned a lot of money and could afford to live magnificently in a villa, and I couldn't. The next day, I called my friend who had taken me to the presentation, and I asked her to explain to me how it worked. She said that she was a newcomer, and that only Thomas could have explained it to me better. He was the man who led the presentation. So I met my mentor and future husband," said Nora.

"And he taught me everything I know about this profession," she added.

It was all very touching for me.

"Well, now, let's just chat," Nora said. "Let's go back to business. What are the first steps you took as a business partner when you started the business? When we start this business, there are several steps you need to follow in order to succeed, which you will then have to repeat again and again. I'll explain to you now," she said.

Find Your "Why" and Choose Your Goal

"And how much do you want to earn?" Nora asked.

"As much as possible," I replied. She smiled.

"No, it won't work. Listen, when you go on vacation, don't tell yourself: 'I'll go on vacation; I'll go somewhere,'" she said.

"Of course not," I replied. "I always plan a vacation," I added. "I always look for a beautiful place by the sea, in a hotel, and I always try to have full board," I explained.

"So, you plan where you will go, and logically, also in which period you will go, right?" asked Nora for confirmation. "Then you plan the conditions in which you want to live, to know how much it will cost, don't you?" she added.

"Yes, exactly!" I confirmed.

"For some reason, many people plan their holidays very seriously, but when it comes to earnings, especially in network marketing, they just say, 'I want to make more money.' This is not a criterion. How much more? Perhaps you will earn an extra euro or 10 euros more. But you're not starting our business for this, right?" She made me think.

"Okay, I understand; I would like to earn at least € 300 the first month from now," I said. "And after 6 months, I would like my earnings to increase by 6 times. I would like to earn € 1800 a month, and after a year, double this amount. Do you think I will succeed?" I asked.

Nora replied, "I cannot give you guarantees that you will earn this money. But if you work, and you follow the steps that I teach you, and you do it actively and regularly, you will have every chance to realize your plan.

"Just tell me if you asked yourself why you need € 1,800 or € 3,600 a month. I don't think so, or if you did, it surely wouldn't have been in the right way, because our brain doesn't perceive money in numbers but in images. If you need € 1800, for example, to buy a new car, this would be a good goal. What kind of car would you like? Can you choose a photo of this machine, find out exactly how much it costs, and maybe even decide on the color? I even advise you to go to the dealer, choose a similar car, sit in this car, and maybe take a driving test, so that your desires are supported not only by logic but also by feelings," she advised me.

"Yes, I would really like to buy a car, and I would also like to travel a lot. I would like to visit America and Australia," I stated.

"Great," said Nora.

"Start writing your dreams as a plan: Earnings this month (note the month and year) € 300 extra. I earn in network marketing, in six months (put the date), € 1800, and I buy a car (brand, model, color, and as many details as possible). Then, after a year (put the date), I earn € 3,600 more, and I go to America.

"Specify where you want to go, what you want to visit, etc. Find photos of what you want to buy or where you want to go, thanks to additional earnings on the Internet. Put them on the desktop of your computer and tablet. Everything has to be real and attractive so that your subconscious starts working toward your goals. When you have clear goals, it is much easier to reach them. Write them on paper and leave them in different places where you will always see them. Every morning and evening, stop and read your goals. Try to view them. And every morning, you decide what you want to do to achieve them. In the evening, think and write what you did during the day to achieve these goals.

"Do it regularly, and let it become a habit. Initially, it is not easy. But let your goals take you to a regular and active job. And you will succeed!" she concluded. Nora patted me on the shoulder.

On my website, www.connectandgrowrichbook.com, you will find a form with which you can make a list of your goals. Download it and note your goals.

Be 100% Sure

Nora started talking, "What do you think, Natalia? What is the most important thing for succeeding in our business?"

I thought for a moment and then answered, "I think it is important to get to know many people, and to know the products well."

"Yup!" Nora smiled. "All this is important, but the most important thing is that you are 100% convinced that your company, your products, your business plan, and your services are the best. It's called motivation," she said.

I remember this conversation with Nora, when I work with business partners or recommend the people who just start this business. They often ask me this question. And in my opinion, being motivated and convinced is the most important thing.

"If you are convinced, motivated, prepared, and talk enthusiastically about your product, you will sell a lot, and you will have many new business partners. If you're trying but can't do it, ask yourself, 'Hey, but am I 100% sure that what I offer is the best?' To succeed in our business, it's not enough to love the product and know it; it is necessary to know all the positive aspects, and to understand why it is better than other products. Furthermore, you need to be

The First Secrets of a Successful Start

sure of your company, business plan, and service. You need to fall in love with your project! Have you ever been in love?" Nora asked.

"Yes," I replied.

"Remember how you spoke, and how you thought of your chosen one? How your eyes shone, how all his qualities were excellent, how he was the best, and you knew perfectly well why it was so? In our sector, it is more or less the same. For success, you have to fall in love with your product, your company, your business plan, and the service you offer. This does not happen once and for all. It is necessary, as in relationships, to keep this feeling alive and always renew it. What are the advantages of our product compared to competitive products? What are the strengths of your company? What is the strength of your compensation plan? What is the strength of the fact that you sell these products and offer services to your customers?

"I know business partners who try, without success. They know how to call people, how to invite, and how to make a presentation, and we'll talk about this soon," said Nora. "But these people are not successful. With careful analysis, we understand that these people have lost their initial enthusiasm. Remember then, along with the skills that I will teach you, that the most important condition for success is a strong confidence in your product, in your company, and in your project. All this will make you strong; it will lead you to success, and no one can stop you," she concluded.

Now, dear reader, let's do an exercise.

Sit down and think about the strengths of your product, your company, your business plan, and the service; take a sheet and write 40 characteristics.

Give yourself 15 minutes, write these 40 characteristics, and then think about each one of them and how you can justify them.

These characteristics will be the basis of your belief and your success.

You can find and download some features, on my site, www.connectandgrowrichbook.com.

Just to give you an idea: The others, you create by yourself. They will help you earn a fortune.

Use the Product and Create Your Story

As you will remember, it is very important that our products are effective, and many companies in network marketing have excellent products. The problem is that the products cannot speak and explain how good they are, and we are paid to just pass on information about the usefulness of these products to our customers and future business partners.

Start immediately to use the product or service that you will offer.

When I talk at presentations or conferences, and meet successful people from all over the world, everyone says they fell in love with the product.

"Therefore, regularly use the product, and carefully observe the improvements made by the product. It is better to write about it, think about it, and create your story," advised Nora. "And what is the best way to tell your own story? Let's look at your story together," she replied, inviting me to begin my story.

"I am an export manager, so I travel a lot for work. I had

come to feel very tired and stressed, and did not sleep well at night. A friend advised me to try the products, and within a week, I began to feel better and much more energetic. In a month, the tiredness completely faded, and now I feel stronger, and I sleep much better too. Even my physical appearance has improved: my skin and my hair. Furthermore, after a while, I began to receive numerous compliments. My friends told me, and they still say, 'I see you are very well! You have such a radiant face! What are you using?'" I told her.

"Good!" Nora began. "You got a nice result. Now imagine that you have been invited to a presentation, and you want to tell your story. Remember the most salient details. Say your name, the place where you live, and your age if you want. Talk about your initial problem, and tell how long you have used the product and what changes have occurred. The story must be brief and emotional. Now, you try."

"My name is Natalia; I have ... (years), and I live in Bolzano (Italy). I am an export manager, so I have to travel a lot for work. I came to feel very tired and stressed, and I didn't sleep well at night. A friend, one day, advised me to try the company's products. I started using them, and within a week, I felt a lot more energy in my body. In one month, my tiredness had completely disappeared, and now I feel strong and I sleep much better. Even my physical appearance has improved: muscle tone, skin, and even hair. I started receiving numerous compliments. My friends say, 'I see you are very well! You have such a radiant face! What are you using?' Thanks to (the company) for excellent products," I concluded. "I understand," I said.

"And it's even better," said Nora, "If you describe your

conditions before starting to take the products. For example, if you feel tired, you don't sleep well, or if you have something sore. I suggest you take a picture, because people often change a lot, but since we see ourselves every day, we do not notice it. It is very effective to use the before and after images when working with weight control, beauty, and skin care products. Think about how many people you can help, who might have the same problem as you. Listen carefully when you meet people who have a good product result, and collect these stories! This will be your capital. You can always tell a story that best fits your potential customer or business partner.

"It is very important that neither you nor your clients use the words in their story (for example, the product cured me of ..., or thanks to the product, I recovered from ...). Our products are not medicines; they do not cure. Perhaps the ingredients they contain help people regain balance in their bodies, but we have no right to say that these products have cured someone of a disease. This is very important! Remember that in network marketing, the stories sell, and people love to hear stories!" she explained.

"Wonderful!" I said.

This means that the main thing is to use the product and create your story.

And now, dear readers, take a notebook, set a stopwatch for 15 minutes, and write your story.

You can find and download an example of a story, on my site, www.connectandgrowrichbook.com.

The First Secrets of a Successful Start

How to React to "No"

"I want to warn you about something important," said Nora, and then she continued.

"In our business, as in any business, you will have good days and bad days. Sometimes people say *no*. Throughout my career, I have received many no's. What is the difference between me and the people who failed in our business? The secret is to have received many no's, but nevertheless, being able to continue working and acting. I analyzed my mistakes; I asked people why they refused, but I never stopped! Many people, who have not achieved success in network marketing, say that this business is not for them, and that they do not have the skills for it, or that the system does not work.

"I know a lot of people all over the world, who, having found the right company, have started working at the right time (timing), and are using the methods I will teach you now. They have achieved enormous success and financial independence. For this, I know for a fact that our business works, and when I analyze the stories of these people, I see that all of them initially were ordinary people. Each of them was either a teacher, a worker, a student, a pensioner, and so on. They had no specific knowledge, talents, or skills. They wanted to make their dreams come true. They loved the product and the company, and they learned this business. But the main thing that probably unites them is their perseverance towards the goal, despite the no's received. Once, I talked to a very successful leader, and he told me how he managed to develop the resistance to the no's that he received.

"Imagine the situation: You prepared a wonderful dish,

and a friend came to you. You really want to eat, and you would like your friend to eat with you. The dish looks good, smells good, and you're sure it's delicious, but your friend refuses to even taste it, saying that he just ate. Wouldn't you be offended, and decide not to invite him again? Or would you never cook again? I guess not. Just say, 'Well, it doesn't matter.' The same happens with our business. When we present our opportunity and our products to friends, acquaintances, and relatives, and for some reason, they say no, we must not be offended or angry. And for sure, we must not stop doing business or start saying that the business does not work, or that something is wrong with us.

"The person who refused probably had their reasons. Maybe they were very busy or didn't understand the opportunity. Perhaps they once tried to work in network marketing and did not achieve success. Maybe they were part of the wrong company, or they weren't taught how to work. Maybe someone told them about their bad experiences, or maybe a person had problems at home or at work, and at the time of the proposal, they couldn't think of anything else. We can ask a person the reason for their refusal, but we must also learn to calmly accept a *no,* to go to the top of our career. This is very important.

"If a person begins to criticize the possibility of network marketing, and to tell bad stories and get discouraged from doing business, stop it. Be nice, but stop it! Tell him: 'I understand your point of view. I am very sorry that this happened to you, but we have a completely different company, so I know I will succeed. How is your son?' Change the subject of the conversation," she explained and suggested.

The First Secrets of a Successful Start

"Don't let anyone convince you that the company, the business, or the product isn't as good as you think. Remember what I told you about the main rule of success: Be 100% convinced! Don't let anyone reduce your confidence. Constantly reinforce it. Learn to accept the no's, and you will get a lot of yes's. Analyze the reasons for the rejection, and try, next time, to make the invitation better. If you don't let the *no* answers stop you, there will be no end to your success!" Nora concluded, transmitting the energy she had in saying all this.

5

What To Do Next

Use, Love, and Explore Your Products

We sat in Nora's office, looking at the lake, and she explained the basics of our business to me. "Now, I will tell you that you will have to do the very beginning, step by step. Remember these actions, perform them regularly, and teach them to your new business partners. This guarantees you a stable and strong business. The first condition, in order to be successful in our business, is to use the products that you sell every day. This is very important, because the most important secret of success, as I have already told you, is to be very confident in your product, your company, and your business. You must become your best customer. You should know your product as no one else knows it. Read everything related to the product, watch the videos, and find customer testimonials. Create your own collection of them!"

Nora continued, "Every time I meet people at conventions or events, and I hear amazing stories about how the product helped, I write down these stories. If possible, I approach them by talking to them, and taking their numbers, or their Facebook contact information. Thus, if I have potential clients who have the same problems, I already have a person who can tell about their result, and help me in selling the product. It is important to also use the product yourself, because we have to be 100% sure of the product. If we have chosen a product that can be ordered every month, how can we ask our customers to order the product again, if we don't do it ourselves? First of all, we should be a good example for ourselves, for our clients, and for our business partners. When you use the product regularly, your confidence grows. You can create an excellent story on the results that the product gives, and take photos before and after using the product. Record all your feelings, and share them with your friends and acquaintances. Remember the number one rule: use, love, and study your product!"

Keep in Touch With the Sponsor

The next day, when I came to Nora, she talked to someone on Skype. She gestured for me to sit down on the sofa and wait.

They spoke German, but I realized that Nora was teaching a new business partner. It was a young woman named Martha. Nora explained to her the importance of being confident in the product, the business, the company, and in herself. She taught the girl to take products regularly, and to create her own story.

She further warned Martha not to lose heart by hearing the word, *no*. Then they agreed on the next meeting on Skype, on the same day, after lunch. The girl had to do some task. The call ended, and Nora greeted me cordially.

"Well," she said. "You have already seen what I do and

What To Do Next

how I advise my business partners to do it. Meet (communicate) with your sponsor regularly. Even if your sponsor or mentor lives far away, this is not a problem. Many people successfully do business through the Internet, or communicate via Skype or other applications. The main thing is to remember that the sponsor is a person who wants to help you and is interested in your success. So try to combine the forces with them, and use their knowledge. If your sponsor is not very experienced, try to work with them anyway, and find, together, the up line person of your organization who wants to help you. Remember, the one alone in the field is not a warrior!

"There is a golden rule of network marketing. Always present your sponsor at its best. I will explain to you how this works. The first people with whom you will be talking about a new opportunity and products will be your friends, relatives, and acquaintances. These people wish us well and love us. But they know us as a good guy or a good girl, and not as an expert in business, products, or services. Therefore, sometimes it will be difficult for them to believe what you are saying. If you present your sponsor as an expert in business and products, and say good words with great respect about him, then your friends will trust you and will listen to him with great attention and respect. After all, they trust you. This is how the human brain works. That is why many prominent personalities always have assistants who represent them.

"When you make your first presentations, try to present your sponsor with the best words. Practice, and think about your words in advance. For example: 'I want to introduce you to a very successful person. He has earned a lot of money; he has been successfully working in business for many years; he has helped so many people; etc.' Then give the floor to the sponsor and let him speak. Let the *third party rule* work. Your acquaintances and friends will listen with great attention to this authoritative person, and with great interest. And the result will be much better. Of course, at the end of the presentation, say to your friends, 'Let's start together!' Or, 'Grandma, please buy a product from me.' Your participation is necessary, but let your sponsor *work*; trust him, and work in a team. This afternoon, you'll see how we do it," said Nora.

Create a List of Contacts

Nora smiled. "Now, remember the golden rule of business success."

"I know, I know!" I exclaimed. "Do everything within the first 72 hours."

"Well done!" Nora said. "As soon as you have decided to start a business, immediately start using the product, call your sponsor, and make an appointment. Meet (even via Skype) with a sponsor, and start working with your capital."

"With my capital?" I was surprised.

"Yes, each of us has our capital," said Nora. "These are people, contacts, and connections that we have built during our life, and which we continue to build. Each average person has about 300 names in his or her phone book. If you are quite young, you may have a few names, but then you probably have a lot of contacts on Facebook. Of course, for our business, we are looking for the sociable, open, and friendly people, who have many contacts and a good reputation. But we'll talk about this later. The main thing now is to start making your contact list.

What To Do Next

"Take a new notebook, specifically for this purpose, and start recording the names of all the people you know. Write the first name, last name, phone number, email, and Facebook contact—in general, how you can communicate with the person. Indicate their age, profession, and how you know each other. For example, they might be a friend from your childhood, or a former colleague. Think of the family members of these people you know, and write down their names so as not to forget about them. Later, you can think about how you can find these people's contacts. For each person, there could be 5–7 members of their family. Think about what the potential could be!

"First, write down your closest relatives, friends, and acquaintances. Sometimes people are embarrassed to contact their closest people, because they think they don't want to sell products to their relatives and friends. But this is the wrong approach. Think about what network marketing can bring you—freedom, wealth, better health and better appearance, right?"

"Yes, of course!"

"This is a real treasure," said Nora.

"I agree," I replied.

"So, why are some people embarrassed to share their treasure with loved ones? If you had found a treasure in your garden, and you would have to dig in the ground to get it, to whom would you go first of all for help? To people whom you know, whom you trust and who trust you, or would you stop a stranger on the street and tell him about the treasure?"

"Of course, I would go to my family members and closest friends."

"It is the same in our business. We can share our

treasure first with the closest people, and they can decide whether they want to take this treasure or not. You also shouldn't make a decision for other people."

"What does it mean?" I asked.

"Well, for example, you think, 'No, I do not want to talk to this person; he or she already earns a lot.' In fact, we are just too shy to talk to people who are more successful than us. Maybe this person wants to earn more, or he doesn't have enough time to communicate with his family. And you have the opportunity to make this possible, so that he'll earn even more, and he'll have time to communicate with his loved ones."

Therefore, within 72 hours from the moment you made a decision, take a notebook, and your phone, and start recording all the people you know, to share with them the real treasure that you just found.

You can find and download a sample of how to create a list of contacts, on my website, www.connectandgrowrichbook.com.

Qualify Your Contacts

I sat on Nora's terrace and wrote out my contacts. An hour passed, and I had written out most of my contacts, although many were still on my phone. Nora, who had just finished a conversation via Skype, with Martha, approached me and asked, "How are you?"

"I'm doing well. What will we do with my contacts?" I asked.

"Now we classify them," she answered. "Think about who you would like to work with."

"With positive, businesslike, fun, interesting people," I

replied.

"Well, then let's classify the people on your list. The first category is potential customers. Think of the benefits that our product gives to customers. Now, go through your list and mark the letter P, for people who may have some kind of health problem with energy or vitality. P means a product, and these people can be your potential customers.

"Now think about the people who would like to make money, who everyone knows, who have a lot of contacts, and who speak different languages. Also, think about those who love to travel, who are open in their minds, or who have already worked in network marketing. These people can be our business partners. Therefore, put in front of them, the letter B (for business)."

I was left alone and quickly placed these letters on my list.

"Next," Nora said, "We will qualify the people you would like to work with. Are there any among them that are better or worse than you, according to some characteristics?"

"Of course, because all people are different."

Nora smiled. "Well, who would you rather work with?"

"With those who are in something better than me."

"That is a wise decision. And now, let's see which of your friends have the highest rating. Try to put points to your friends, from one to ten. The highest score will be given to people with characteristics that we just talked about: openness to new things; a positive outlook; a lot of contacts, including abroad; having experience in network marketing; and so on. The more similar characteristics a person has, the higher his rating is in our qualification. If this person is negative, with the consciousness of a poor man who constantly complains, his rating will be very low.

I would not like to work with such people," Nora said. "You probably wouldn't either. But this person can still be informed. He may not be ready for our opportunity or product, but he may know someone and point you to this person. You just do not need to focus on negative people; do not convince anyone—just give them the information. Of course, we will start to contact people with the highest rating. More often than not, it is these people who are open to everything new. They want to try a product or start a new business, and try a new opportunity. Therefore, it is very important to include all of your friends in the list of people, and to qualify this list."

You can find and download the list of characteristics that determine the high rating of a person's contact list, on my website, www.connectandgrowrichbook.com.

Invite, Invite, Invite

"Well, now, when you have written and qualified your contact list, we will begin the most important work that a new business partner should do. It is to invite people. Have you ever organized a party or invited friends to go with you to dinner?"

"Of course," I said.

"We will do the same now. Remember how you invite friends?"

I replied, "That's very simple: 'Hi, how are you? Are you free Friday night? Let's go eat pizza together and chat.'" (Do not forget that I had then lived in Italy, so the most popular pastime was to go out and eat pizza.)

Nora laughed. "I would immediately agree! You should invite people to the presentation of the product or business in this mode. Many new distributors are so excited about the new project, and they want to get a result sooner, so they start calling their friends and telling them by phone about the project or product. This shouldn't be done! Our task is to invite a person so that he spends a little time and attention, and is told about the project or product. It is better if this is done by a person who presents as an expert. People listen to experts much more attentively than to their friends or relatives. Soon, I will show you how to invite. The main thing is to agree in advance with your sponsor, where and when you want to invite people. As Brian Tracy, a well-known business coach, said: 'Know your goal initially.'

"What should be the purpose of your call? Sell a product? No! Find a new business partner? No! The purpose of your call is an invitation to a presentation, a webinar, or a meeting with your sponsor (including a Skype meeting). There, your potential client or partner will be told everything about the project, product, and business. Do not turn the invitation into a presentation. And try to make as many invitations as possible. This will help you become a true master. Remember professional athletes. After all, they achieve excellent results, not only because they have remarkable abilities, but because they spend a lot of time in training. The same goes for our business. To work out the skill of inviting people, you need to train. So, invite, invite, invite!"

How to Invite People

"And now, I'll tell you how to invite people," Nora told me. "It's very simple. There are some rules to follow. I advise you to always have a script with you," she stated, and then handed me a sheet.

"What are they?" I asked.

"Always call with great energy, in an enthusiastic mood, and be a little excited and always in a hurry. Make it clear that you have very little time, but what you are saying is very important. It is better to make calls while standing up, using earphones, so that you can even gesticulate—sometimes it helps. There are several steps to follow, which I will now show you as a numbered list."

1) Hello (friend's name). I am (your name).

"Why is it also important to say your name?

It is very unpleasant when someone calls us and we do not recognize the person by the voice, and this person continues to talk, not telling who he is. This creates embarrassment. Therefore, it is better to pronounce your name immediately."

2) How are you? How is your family? How are the children? The dog? How's work? Everything is alright?

"This is the so-called small talk. Here, we give the person some time to share the news with us. What is his mood; how is he? If he is ill, and he answered us without much strength, then it makes no sense to invite him now to the presentation, or to tell him of our wonderful business at that time. Suffice it to say that we feel sorry for him, wish him a quick recovery, and say that as soon as he can, it is very important for us to talk to him, because we have something very interesting for him.

If the person is fine, then you can proceed to the next step of the call."

3) Are you free? Do you have a couple of minutes for me?

"It is important to check availability. Because if a person

is at work and cannot speak, he does not pay us the necessary attention.

When he answers, 'Yes, I can talk,' take the next step.

If they don't have time, you can say: 'Okay, I'm in a hurry too. When can I call you back? It's an important thing.' Mark the time he indicates, and call at that time."

4) (Name of the friend), I'm calling you for a very important reason. A few days ago, I met a person who came to our city and showed me a business project. Remember, some time ago, when we talked about how it would be nice to make more money, because you want to buy a new car? So, this man showed me the opportunity of how we can earn together without giving up our job. I want to share this information with you. Imagine how you could buy a new car, and we could ride in it together! We definitely need to do this one of these days. I want to introduce you to this wonderful person while he is in our city."

5) When can we meet? What about Tuesday or Thursday night?

"Now we have to offer the person two options of when and where we can see each other. A person should always have a choice.

The friend could answer: 'On Thursday, I am free.'"

6) Confirmation: 'Great! Then let me pick you up Thursday at 7:00 pm, and we'll meet this person together, okay?'

'Okay.'

7) 'Excellent! See you Thursday at seven. Mark it on the calendar; I already did it. I am sure you will like it.'

'All right, see you Thursday!'

"This is the greeting phase. It is important to greet with

a smile, and quickly, before the friend starts asking us questions."

I asked Nora, "And what happens if my friend says, 'But could you explain to me what it is?'"

"In that case," she said, "Answer."

'Sure, that's why I want to see you. I want to introduce you to the person who told me about this opportunity. He has a lot of experience, he has already helped many people earn extra money, and he is simply an exceptional person. So, do you prefer Tuesday or Thursday night?'

Answer: 'On Thursday, I am free."

If the person insists: 'But explain it to me anyway; what is it?'

Say: 'Listen, it's about how to earn more money, but it seems to me that this is not particularly interesting for you, so forget it. I'll see you for a coffee, and have a chat. It's been so long since we've seen each other. This is an opportunity only for those who really want to make more money.'

And say goodbye: 'Bye, I'm in a hurry; see you.' We don't need to convince and persuade anyone! We just have to invite," she warned me.

"The most important thing is to prepare well. Keep the script in front of you, and a list that includes the strengths of your business, your product, and your company. It is very important to be brief. Do not start a presentation but simply invite. When people ask additional questions, answer briefly and clearly. And remember: the more invitations you make, the better you will become at inviting, and the more people will know your product and your business. See this task as an athlete who trains before a competition, and you will become a true champion!" suggested Nora.

What To Do Next

You can find an example of an invitation script on my site, www.connectandgrowrichbook.com.

And according to the rules, you can create your own script.

6

Several Ways To Do Business

The First Appointments With Your Sponsor

"Now," said Nora, "You know how to invite people, and you have to do some practice. The best thing to do is to meet with your sponsor as soon as possible, and set up your first appointments. It is best to do this within 48 or 72 hours from the beginning of your activity. Remember the rule of successful people!

"If your sponsor lives at a distance, establish a Skype call with him or her. Read aloud the script you have prepared, with the help of your sponsor, or the script that he himself gave you. Read it aloud, repeat it, and study it by heart. For a while, you become an actor who plays a part. But until you have learned the script by heart, always keep it in front of you. Decide with your sponsor when you do the presentations together. Ninety percent of people have started working in network marketing as a part-time job. Ask your sponsor or up line when he or she is available (days and times) to help you. Try to get rid of all social commitments on these dates. By doing so, your sponsor will also see that you are seriously interested and are taking this commitment as a serious matter. When you have established the days and time, decide which type of presentation you want to do.

"Surely, to start well and to have some training, the best thing to do is organize a launch evening or an inauguration of your business. Decide on the date within the first week of activity, and when you could invite your closest relatives and friends to your home. Call them, and explain to them that you have started a new part-time business, and that you would like to introduce them to the company, the products, and the person who introduced you to this project."

"Soon," she said, "We go to Martha, and you will have the chance to see how you can organize this evening. The important thing is to always plan it with your sponsor, and to do it as soon as possible. You can even do two or three evenings during the same week, always using the invitation script I told you about earlier. Now, let's get ready and go to Martha's house. I warned her that you are coming with me, and she will be happy to meet you," said Nora.

Launch Evening or Business Opening

We arrived at Martha's house, in a suburb near Zurich. In Switzerland, they have dinner early, so Martha had called her friends and a couple of relatives to join her after dinner. Nora explained that Martha had invited guests by phone, 2–3 days earlier. Soon after, she told the girl to call her guests or send them a message a day earlier to remind them of the event, and to ask them to be punctual.

Martha and her parents welcomed us in a very polite and friendly manner. Her mom said she was very curious about what it was, and Nora assured her that she would explain it all a little later.

Martha led us into the living room. Everything was ready for the presentation. Everything was in order, and the seats were ready: a big sofa, a couple of armchairs, and two chairs, in case someone else arrived. In the middle, there was a table with the products of our company, along with samples, brochures, some other sheets (they were the customer profile cards, but the text could not be seen), and a vase of fruit. Next to a large TV was Martha's PC, attached to it to project videos. The atmosphere was welcoming; Martha also had flowers and some music. Nora and Martha agreed that Nora would arrive a little earlier than the guests. Martha had also prepared a refreshing drink, some saltines, and some fruit cut up on a tray. When the first guests started arriving, we welcomed them with smiles. Martha accommodated the guests, and when they all arrived, she presented Nora as a very successful and experienced person. In all, there were 7 people. The presentation started almost on time.

Martha began by saying that she had met her sponsor, Nora, and that she had great success in this business.

Martha told her story and showed pictures of her face, before and after using the products. Initially, she had impure skin, while now, she had a beautiful appearance. Her relatives and friends nodded. They saw the differences, as they knew the girl well. Then Martha passed the word to Nora, and explained that Nora had presented the products. Our mentor started with a few jokes; people smiled and asked her a few questions. It seemed that these people knew her, despite it being the first time they had made her acquaintance. Nora told her story, talked about the company, and started the company video on the products. She had done it on purpose: She could have explained the products herself, but she wanted everything to be simpler and easier to duplicate for her new collaborator.

After the video, she asked people if they had any questions, and they started asking something. Martha and I offered them samples of the products to try. Here, the fun part began. Everybody started trying samples, and they said they liked the taste, and asked more questions. Nora replied, and Martha and I listened. Nora explained that they could try the products as customers of Martha, or become her business partners, to get more advantageous prices and the chance to earn. She said that those interested in this option could talk to her and Martha the next day, on another occasion. A couple of Martha's friends made an appointment with Nora.

Everything happened as if by magic. The parents, aunt, and a friend of the girl wanted to try the products, and immediately placed the order online. Martha had found her first customers. And her other friends, the next day, became her collaborators, having been interviewed by Nora via Skype. Martha was very happy.

Returning from Martha's evening, Nora said:

"This is the most effective way to start the business and get the first results."

The Business Meeting

"And now, we will talk about the business meeting," said Nora, "which has always been a very effective method in network marketing. Perhaps in your city, there are already business meetings, or if you have some experience, and you have a group, you can create a meeting of your own. The advantage of a business meeting is the possibility of speaking on one occasion with many people. It is also an excellent opportunity to train your skills as a public speaker. Many people are afraid to speak in public. Speaking at a meeting, you have the possibility to do the practice, starting with 10 or 15 minutes. The business meetings usually take place in very nice hotels, like four-star hotels and up. The network marketing company must have a certain image, especially if we talk about the opportunity of a big business. If you have decided to attend an event, remember some rules. Dress appropriately, with clothes a little more elegant than usual. It doesn't have to be an expensive or signature suit, but it has to be elegant, fairly new, and cared for. You have to stand out. Do not overdo cosmetics, perfume, and jewelry, even if you like them so much. You have to look nice and professional. As a business partner, you come a little earlier than the guests. Help prepare the room. Contribute to the room, because the business meeting is for everyone. But above all, it is important to have the right attitude! Yes, smiling and friendly, and if for some reason you do not have guests, welcome the guests of the others with enthusiasm, because the others will do the same with your guests in the future.

"Have your guests sit in the meeting room, introduce them to successful people, and build up the sponsor or up line. When the presentation begins, pay attention to the speaker. Don't browse Facebook, and don't reply to messages, because your guests are watching you and doing the same. Would you like your guest to listen carefully? Then do the same. Even if the speaker is not very experienced or, because of the emotion, he made some blunders, pretend nothing happened, nod, and give him support. Your guests will not notice the error. It is important to create a positive atmosphere. It is not always easy. Sometimes when your guest does not arrive, and you are angry with him or even disappointed, you must have your feelings under control. Always remember that network marketing is a long-term business that allows you to have passive earnings for years and even decades. Just decide to invite even more people next time, and have lots of guests. Don't be discouraged by obstacles. Keep your goal in mind, and succeed.

"Remember, people are watching you, even when you don't notice. For this reason, please use positive language, be smiling and friendly, and be kind to everyone. This is the right attitude in business meetings, and in life in general."

Skype and Zoom Call

"Another very effective tool is Skype," said Nora. "You can also use Zoom or another application. Why are they so effective? Because you can give a presentation to a person or a group of people, at any time, in any location. You can invite your sponsor or up line. The effectiveness of this method is that you can share the screen and show slides, documents, your back office, and your Internet site to your potential client or collaborator. It is also an interactive tool because people usually see themselves, and they like it a lot. Although this method is online, you can talk to people and see their reactions to what you are saying. You can ask questions or answer their questions, and this makes the presentation much more effective.

"Surely, sitting next to your potential customer in a living room is the ideal thing, but if the person lives far away, this method is excellent: You don't have to waste time on the journey; you don't have to spend the money on gasoline; the Internet connection is almost free, and everyone has it. For this reason, it is a very useful and even duplicable tool. Every person who has Internet, a tablet, or a computer, and has an hour a day, can do this business directly from home or from their office. This method is ideal for those who say: 'But I have no time.' It is important, during the presentation, to ask lots of questions, to make sure that our interlocutor is with us and is following us. It is obvious that a good Internet connection is also important. It is best to warn the person that it is preferable that he or she is in a quiet place, where he/she is not disturbed during the half hour or 40 minutes, in which the opportunity is explained. I happened to invite people to a Skype call and, in the background, the family dined, the children screamed, or the TV was on. In these conditions, the person is distracted. The important thing, to be able to make a good presentation, is to have the attention of our guest.

"The invitation to a Skype call is the same as a meeting invitation. We can ask: 'On Tuesday or Thursday night, are you usually at home? Great, then I invite you to see something. Do you use Skype? Download it; it's free.'

"You can also say: 'Let me introduce you to an extraordinary person who introduced me to this project. What is your name in Skype? Great, this person is called ... Accept it among your contacts, please. Perfect, I'll see you on Skype, on Thursday at 8.00pm,'" Nora explained.

"Remember to send a reminder in the afternoon before the event, and a message, 10 minutes before asking, 'Are you already at home? Is your Skype working?' The algorithm is the same one you saw at Martha's home," said Nora. "The new collaborator greets his guest, tells his story about the product or activity, if he has it, and presents his sponsor by acknowledging him/her. The sponsor does the rest. In the final part, the new collaborator can ask his guest, 'Beautiful, right? Do you want to start with me?'

The important thing, after finishing the presentation, is to answer the questions and ask the guest what decision he would like to make. In case he or she still has questions, make another appointment within 72 hours," concluded Nora.

One-to-One Presentation

"The most effective method," said Nora, "is the one-to-one presentation. I recommend making the first presentations with the participation of your sponsor. Or you could call your sponsor and have him talk to your friend during the presentation, to give his testimony. You must notify the sponsor first, of course.

"The invitation to the one-to-one presentation is as we said earlier. You have to think before choosing the place where you want to do this presentation. You could go to your friend's house if you are in confidence. Even if the spouse or partner is at home, it is so much better, because you won't hear the excuse, 'I have to talk to my husband/wife.' If you know the person well and have a nice home, you can invite the person to your home. For people who are not in your close circle of friendship, propose to meet them in the lobby or bar of a nice hotel in your city, or in a coffee shop or restaurant. The important thing is that the place is not too crowded and noisy, and that it is a nice place, because it presents a great company and opportunities. Try to get to the meeting, in a public place, a little earlier than your guest. Choose a quiet place, without distractions: television, loud music. Try to sit with your back to the wall. This is the position of strength and security. Prepare yourself well for each interview: computer, presentation, samples, price list, brochures, and everything you need to make a good presentation. Be professional and be prepared!

"Welcome your guest with a smile, in a cordial manner. Have a chat and try to find out what the person's problems are right now. Health problems? Problems at work? Maybe your friend is not happy with their current job? Perhaps he/she is a separate person who would like to make new friends? Listen carefully to what the person tells you. After talking for a while, say that you called the person to show her/him this opportunity. Ask how much time your friend has. If he/she says that they have half an hour, then that is perfect. Thus, you know that you will have to give a presentation for half an hour. Usually, all companies have an official presentation. Follow the slides, and tell your story about the product or earnings. Be simple and be yourself. If you have product samples, let them try the product, and see if the person likes it. At the end of the presentation, answer the questions, and if you can't answer, don't get upset. Simply tell the person:

'I don't have the answer because I just started. But I can verify and give you the answer as soon as possible.' Ask the person if he/she wants to try the products, or if he/she is interested in the business. Always ask your guest which product or products he/she would like to start with. Most companies nowadays have online shops, so go to your shop or back office, and complete the sale or register a new business partner. If the person still has questions, answer them. If you don't have the answer, ask:

'If I answer these questions, would you be ready to make your decision?' If the answer is yes, set another appointment within 72 hours, and look for answers.

"Remember, if you do a presentation a day, and work five days a week, there are five presentations a week, and 20 presentations a month. Do you think that by making 20 presentations a month, you can find some customers or business partners?" she asked.

"Sure!" I said.

"Now, think about duplication. When you have new business partners, and they, too, will start giving presentations, your time and results will be duplicated. This is the strength of network marketing," Nora stated in conclusion.

Webinar or Call

"Today, we are very busy, and sometimes people don't want to go out after work. Or you may have people who live far away from you. This, however, should not stop you from giving them information," said Nora.

"In the modern era, we have fantastic tools, like the webinar, which we can use every day. There are people in my organization," Nora continued, "who even use it three times a day, every day, for seven days a week. This method is very convenient, especially for those who take shifts, work in the evening, and cannot participate in any event or meeting during the day or evening. The webinar is an online presentation. We use a platform, and there are many: GoToWebinar.com, or ClickMeeting.com, and many others. It could be that your company has already set up a webinar, and you just need to start inviting people. When you have more experience, you could do your own webinar or ask someone from your team to do it together. A webinar can also be registered. The important thing is to invite people to this event.

"From experience," suggested Nora, "it is better to ask if the person is available at that time of day, but do not immediately give the link. In the initial invitation, you could also say that you have the possibility to invite only two people and, therefore, it is important for you to be sure that the invited person will be there. Five to six hours before the webinar call, send a reminder message to the person, and tell them that you will be sending a link half an hour before the event. Remember to send the link half an hour before, and 10 minutes before the webinar, send them a message and ask: 'Did you receive the link? Have you tried to connect? Does it work?' This is so that the person has time to connect and listen carefully. Say also, to the person, that you will call him/her after the webinar to know his/her opinion, and to answer any questions.

"This method works great, especially if you can put your potential client or collaborator in contact with your sponsor or up line. At this point, you two would be talking to your guest. Remember always to present your sponsor in an excellent manner. Have your sponsor answer your candidate's questions. Write the answers. The questions are repeated often so you can learn faster. I know a lot of people who entered the business or became customers thanks to a webinar and a three-way call after this event.

"Some companies also organize company calls with the

company leader. This method is also very effective, especially if, afterwards, your potential client is called by you, and you present your sponsor to him/her. As you can see, you can do this business in various ways, working intelligently," Nora concluded.

7

How To Be the Best in Follow-Up

Why Do You Need To Have Follow-Up?

"Now, I want to talk to you about follow-up," Nora said. Network marketing is different from traditional business, in that follow-up is perhaps the most important part of the job. After all, our products do not sell in stores, supermarkets, or in the distribution network. Because they can be found only by people who are partners of the company, these are exclusive products. The company wants people to get results from its products or services. Therefore, the company pays us, the business partners, because we should not only find customers but also help them achieve results.

"A great many people in our industry achieve success and have a good base of regular customers, as they care about follow-up. There are also a huge number of people who have begun network marketing, and then they left it, complaining that they constantly need to look for customers, that no one wants to buy products from them, and so on. In fact, they simply did not pay attention to the follow-up that they had. After all, our clients are our main capital. If we serve them well, and they get excellent results thanks to the products and our service, they will definitely recommend someone else to us. This person can become a client or business partner. We will talk about this later. Have you ever bought some cream or perfume in a pharmacy?"

"Yes, I have," I replied.

"You hardly ever got a call from the store the next day, asking how you liked their product, how you used it, or if you were satisfied. It would be very strange if employees of traditional outlets did this, right? And we, as network marketing partners, are doing just that. We advise the product, and when a person buys it from us, we make sure that he/she likes the product, gets the result, leaves us a wonderful review, and introduces us to other people. Isn't that great?" Norah asked with a smile. "As Jim Rohn said, 'If you make a sale, you can make a living. If you make an investment of time and good service in a customer, you can make a fortune.' When I conduct trainings with my business partners, or just with people who want to succeed in business, I always emphasize the importance of follow-up."

When To Start Follow-Up

"Follow-up starts from the moment we sell the products. Of course, we work in the business of people, so I also keep in touch with those people who have not yet bought the product and said that it is not interesting. I do the same thing with people I told about the business. The situation of people often changes, so if a person was not interested or did not have the opportunity to buy something from us, perhaps after a while, if we stay in contact and maintain friendly relations, he or she will want to try. Never burn bridges!

"And now," said Nora, "imagine that you sold the product and you need to start servicing a new customer. Some business partners do not care at all about serving their customers, and this is a big mistake.

"Be sure to stay in touch with the person; regularly contact him or her. To find out whether the product has come, whether the person has begun to take it, whether they liked the taste, and so on, I recommend staying in contact with the new client for the first two weeks, almost every day."

"Do I really have to call him or her every day?" I exclaimed.

"Of course not," Nora replied. "Be creative: On the first day, you can call the person; secondly, send him or her a message; and on the third day, send an e-mail with some useful information; on the fourth, video; on the fifth day, call again; and so on. Stay in touch. In addition, try to know the person as best you can. Write down everything about him or her: the names of his family members, especially children; their achievements, birthdays, and outstanding dates. Imagine how nice it is for a person to receive greetings from you on his or her birthday, or on the day their son or daughter gets a diploma. Of course, this requires organization, but when it becomes a habit, it is not at all difficult. Now there are so many programs that help keep contacts in order. And when you start earning more, find someone who can help you with this: a student or a retired person. Give the person ready-made scripts, and let him help you with this. But first, you can do all this yourself. The main thing is to remember that people are our main capital, and we must take care of them and create long-term relationships."

You can find scripts on how to serve your customers, and download them, from my site.

How To Get the Great Testimonials

"Would you like to have a lot of feedback from satisfied customers?" Nora asked.

"Yes, of course," I replied. "But I noticed that people, even if they are very satisfied with the products, for some reason, do not leave their feedback with me. What do I do?"

"And how do you ask for testimonial?" Nora asked.

"I say: 'Listen, I see that you are satisfied with the products and got an excellent result. Could you write a testimonial for me?' The customer says: 'Yes, of course,' but almost never does this."

"I will teach you," Nora said. "Firstly, this problem will not happen if you conduct good follow-up. If you are in constant contact with your customers, and help them understand the benefits and results that your product has given them, this problem is solved very quickly. Many people do not like to write, or are very busy. Therefore, when carrying out follow-up, I fix the improvements that the client told me at the time of our communication. I put it on paper. Do you remember when we talked about how to create your story?"

"Yes, I remember."

"You do the same thing with your customers. Write a story for them:

My name is ... I live in the city ... I started taking the

product because I had (problems that the client has). I have been taking products for two weeks, one month, etc. During this time, I felt (the improvements, the results that the client received).

The next time you call or write to your client, say: 'Listen, as I understand, you are very pleased with the products and the results, right?'"

'Yes,' the client answered.

"'I wrote down your story, the problems that you felt, and the improvements you received using the products. Can I show you this? If you like it and you agree, can you sign this review? Maybe you want to write something else?'

"You can also ask if the client allows you to use your feedback on your website, on your Facebook page, and so on. Also ask if the client could confirm his feedback if you have a potential client with the same characteristics that the client had before trying the product. For example, fatigue, apathy, and so on. Most people will agree, because they are satisfied with the product, and you have a good relationship. And you will see how many excellent reviews from satisfied customers you get!"

Referrals: How To Get Them in Any Situation

"Referrals can be obtained from everyone," Nora said, when we walked along the lake. "The great thing about our business is that you can even get a referral from a person who is not interested in a product or business. When you talk with someone, just say: 'I work with a very large project, with serious entrepreneurs, and we do... (Say in brief what the company does or what business it is in). I am new in this region. Do you know someone who would like to receive additional income? Or who would like to try a new exclusive product for free? I need testimonials from people in this region.' A person will think a little and can tell you: 'My cousin recently told me that he would like to start a business. He is an intelligent man.' Or, they could say: 'I want to try. Exclusive, you say?' Or they may say, 'I don't even know; I have to think.' Take his contact information from him, and tell him that you will call him back in two days. Remember, the rule is 72 hours.

"When you give a presentation, regardless of its outcome, before saying goodbye, be sure to ask the person a question: Who among your acquaintances might be interested in our products? And who among your friends may be interested in additional earnings? A person, especially if he hasn't bought anything from you, is likely to leave you a couple of contacts.

"Yes, it really works! At the very beginning of my work in network marketing, I met one acquaintance who did not want to do business, but when I asked him to introduce me to someone who might be interested, he gave me the names of two of his friends, with telephone numbers. I called these people and then made a Skype call, because they lived far away. Both of them started doing business, made a great career, earned a lot of money, and helped me earn.

"Remember, always, before saying goodbye to a person, to ask for referrals. And, of course, ask for referrals from your clients. If you constantly communicate with them, then you will surely know about their family members: brothers, sisters, parents, and children. All of them can be potential customers or business partners. So, just ask your customers: 'Which of your relatives, friends, or acquaintances could like our products? And which of your friends may be interested in additional earnings?' And you will see how many new contacts you will have!"

How To Engage Customers in the Sales Process

Nora told me, "If your client is pleased with the results, and may have told you that his friends have already asked him what he does in order to be more energetic and so on, ask him to organize a small party or brunch at his home, with friends and relatives. Ask him if he can invite these people, telling them that this will be a party dedicated to wellness, for example. Let him tell them that his guest will be a person who is an expert in a healthy lifestyle. And this expert will tell you how to be fit and feel better. Let them bring nothing, but tell them to be punctual. Come to the meeting a little earlier, and bring your products, samples, brochures and catalogs. Practically, you will spend the evening launching a new business partner. You just do it for your client. Pay more attention to the product, and in the end, you can say that if someone is interested in receiving additional earnings, then you can meet separately.

"Undoubtedly, this meeting will bring a lot of sales. This is logical, because close people have already seen positive changes in the health or appearance of your client. Ask him to tell about his experience with the product. These people trust your client, so finding new customers in this situation will be very easy. Think in advance how you want to reward your client. Calculate the minimum amount new customers should spend to get him a gift. Ask the client if he wants to get a gift or if he wants to make money. For example, if during the evening, customers bought goods for 300 €, you can make a client a gift from your products, for 10% of this amount. Or tell him that he can get this money as an earning if he wants to become a business partner. Listen to what your client says, and act according to circumstances.

"At the end of the evening, be sure to thank your client and new clients. Solemnly present a gift if the customer has chosen this option. Take the names and phone numbers, as well as emails from all participants. Prepare a short questionnaire about what products they liked the most. You can say that you want to stay in touch to send them interesting information, to the code of new products, etc. The main thing is that they get into the database of your potential customers, and you have begun to communicate. Well, those people who bought something will enter your follow-up program, and you will, of course, build good, trusting, long-term relationships with them."

How To Reward the Best Customers

In our times, people are very busy; everyone is in a hurry, and there are very few satisfied people. Have you noticed it?" Nora asked.

"Yes, it is true," I replied.

"Therefore," continued Nora, "people crave recognition and gratitude. Do not forget about it. Try to thank and reward your best customers. What do the best customers mean? This is when people continue to order a product for several months, or bring you other customers, and give you positive feedback and referrals. How can we thank them?

"Prepare a letter of thanks, or an honorary diploma. You

can give a loyal customer a birthday product or a set of samples. Try to organize an event once every three months for your clients. Maybe you will invite a doctor, a cosmetologist, or another specialist who will tell your clients even more about the benefits of the products, and give them some useful information. Try to hold a lottery, or some kind of competition. People love to have fun! You can give honorary diplomas or memorable souvenirs to everyone. Give thanks to your customers. Ask them to invite their friends, relatives, and acquaintances to this meeting. After the event, it would be great to make a small buffet. People love to chat when they have a snack together. You can organize it with your team. And of course, they can invite their customers, and the result will be wonderful for everyone."

It's time to say goodbye to Nora and her husband. I was very grateful to them for their knowledge and advice. I promised myself that I would definitely apply this knowledge and turn it into action. After all, knowledge without action is a road to nowhere. We warmly said goodbye, and I left.

I also promised myself that I would pass this knowledge on to all my business partners, and all the people who will come to my trainings for my consultations. I did not know then that I would write a book. But now, when I write it, I pass on the knowledge that I gained, and the experience that I gained as a result of actions, to you, my dear reader.

The next few months, I spent in active work, and I learned a lot and achieved a lot. In just a few months, our team has grown and strengthened, and we have created a huge turnover. My business colleagues and I achieved high ranks in the company and made a lot of money. We have helped so many people earn and feel better. Business grew, and we continued to work, but I felt that in order to move to the next level of success, it was time to turn to another mentor.

8

How To Reach the Next Level

Meet Markus

Some months passed, and my business started to take off, and I was very happy. My customers were happy with the products and kept re-ordering them. Even my network grew. New people went into business, grew up, earned money, and made a career. I saw that the teachings of my two mentors worked; they had helped me a lot. But I am an ambitious person and felt that I still needed a piece of the puzzle to make the big leap in quality. I went to a corporate event in Orlando. It was a wonderful experience. There, I met another person in my up line, and I realized that this person could have the right answers for me.

Markus was a very experienced person in network marketing, having worked in the industry for over twenty years; but above all, I liked his personality. He was a tall, blond man, with blue eyes, and was in excellent physical shape. It reminded me of James Bond, in his custom-made clothes. I approached him during the event and asked him if I could ask him a few questions, because I wanted to achieve real success in network marketing. The program of the event was very busy for this, and he asked me after the event if I would return immediately to Italy or stay a few more days in America. I had planned to stay there another three days, as I wanted to explore the interesting things that the area offered, and do some shopping. However, when the opportunity presented itself to talk to a guru and discover the secrets of success, I could undoubtedly change my plans and take advantage of this golden opportunity. Markus lived in Miami, which is around 3/4 hours from Orlando. He told me that I could come to visit him in Miami and ask him any questions that were of interest to me. I thanked him; he had inspired me a lot, and I couldn't wait to join him in Miami.

I drove to Miami Beach and reached the beautiful Lakeview area. There were amazing villas of numerous celebrities. I stopped in front of a very modern villa, surrounded by palm trees, and thought: what a wonderful life you can create by starting in such a simple way. I rang the bell. A man came to open the door and made me wait in a nice living room, and then accompanied me to a large attic with a panoramic view, where Markus and his assistant were working on a presentation. They kindly invited me to join them. I was a little intimidated. Everything was so luxurious! The first man, the butler, asked me if I would like something to drink. I took an orange juice and couldn't wait to start talking with Markus. We talked a little about the event we had taken the previous day, and about prominent speakers and important news that had been announced. Markus also asked about my family, and I told him my story.

Afterwards, I sat down with my new mentor, in his studio on the ground floor, and started talking about success.

The Four Characteristics of Successful People

"Markus," I asked, "once I read that to be successful you have to become a successful person. What do you think are the characteristics of a successful person?"

Markus reflected for a while and then asked me, "Have you ever seen James Bond movies?"

"Yes," I said.

"If you look carefully, every successful person is a bit of a James Bond."

"In what sense?" I asked.

"Every successful person has the four characteristics that agent 007 has."

"And what would they be?" I asked.

"Every successful person has security and courage. If you remember, in every movie, James Bond faces the danger and is sure of himself and of what he does. It is always in action. Even a successful business partner is sure of the company and the product, and they believe in themselves and are always in action. To have success, create massive actions. If he must call, he never calls 2–3 people; he calls many. If he has to make presentations, he makes many. Do you understand? A successful business partner does not fear rejection and is not afraid of obstacles," he explained.

"It's true," I agreed.

"The second quality of James Bond is the control of one's emotions. If you read biographies or watch films about the great leaders of the past and present, they all have great self-control. They manage their emotions excellently. This feature must be learned in order to become a great leader of network marketing," he said.

I wrote everything down and reflected on my character, and decided to keep my emotions under control.

"A successful person is also a disciplined person. Self-control and self-discipline help these people to have great results. The third characteristic of the 007 agent is that it unites successful people, and is attentive to their physical form. He is trained, strong, and muscular. It doesn't matter if you are a man or a woman. If you want to be a successful person, you must have a great physique: strong, trained, and agile. You must be prepared not only physically but also mentally. To be fit, you also need to follow a healthy lifestyle: eat healthy; and eliminate bad habits, such as alcohol and smoking. You must be an example because people watch you and copy you.

"The fourth, and last, characteristic that successful people and James Bond have in common is their quality wardrobe. How do you present yourself to people? Do you look like a successful person? Do you remember what James Bond dressed like? He wore elegant clothes made of fine fabrics, and they were made to measure. Now, I'm not saying that you have to have all your clothes made to measure, but pay more attention, from now on, to how you dress. Whether you like it or not, people will take you more seriously if you improve your way of introducing yourself. These 007 traits are great for your life and your business," he concluded.

Have security, self-control, be physically and mentally fit, and create a quality wardrobe to choose from every morning. You will feel better about yourself and become more productive in life, and increase your income.

Take Massive Actions

We were walking with Markus on the waterfront. The weather was fantastic. It occurred to me again that he definitely lives the life of his dreams. I wanted to get there too. I reflected a bit and started asking him questions.

"But what do I do if people tell me: 'I have no time; I have no money; and I am not brought up for network marketing?' It seems to me that I cannot combine much."

Markus looked at me and asked, "But are you sure you are convinced of the project, the product, and the business? Are you sure 110%?"

"Yes," I said. "I'm sure."

"Then you have to increase your actions. How many contacts do you make per day, and how many presentations?" he asked.

I thought for a moment. "From five to seven calls, two or three appointments, and a meeting a week," I replied.

"Here is the answer to your question!" exclaimed Markus. "You miss massive actions. Remember that we are an example, and if we do two or three presentations a day, our team will do even less. For this reason, be an example for others and for yourself. Fill your days. Some think that money makes happiness. It is not really so. Yes, money is convenient, and money makes your life more comfortable, but it doesn't make you happier. It is only actions with production that make you feel good and be satisfied. Try from now on to fill your days with actions that will bring you profits. We will see which ones are ahead. The important thing is that you understand the principle and remember to observe it. Increase your actions at least 10 times, and you will see that your life and your results will change dramatically," he suggested.

"But how do I do it?" I asked Markus. "I work all day; I have a child, and I can dedicate maybe two hours a day to network marketing. On Saturdays, I can do a few more hours. And the same is true of all my collaborators," I explained.

"Two hours per day!?" he stated. "But it's a lot. The important thing is that when you do something, you focus on what you do. When I do something, I don't do it individually, but always massively. When I decide to make phone calls, I immediately make a block of 10 or 20. When I decide to make new contacts, I make dozens of them. When I present the opportunity or product to people, I try to talk to as many people as possible at the same time. I use the webinar, Skype, to organize meetings. In your case, if you have the Saturday, you can dedicate to the activity. In your place, I would schedule appointments one after the other. You can also invite a couple of people at a time. If one does not show up, do not waste your time. And if they come in twos, you can always say, 'Hi guys; so many people are interested in our project that I have to bring people together in groups. Otherwise, I don't have enough time,'" Markus advised me.

"Now it's clear to me," I said. "I have to act massively!"

Actions That Bring Earnings

Markus continued, "There are people who seem to do a lot. They are constantly busy but do not have the results. These people make a mistake. It seems that they have massive actions, but these actions do not bring gains. When planning your day and your week, be careful that your actions are 90% those that will bring you profits. These actions are: calls, presentations, and the creation of new contacts."

"Who do you have to call? Your potential customers and your potential business partners. Follow up and call existing customers, and also current business partners. It is very important to maintain contact with the people in your organization, especially with new and more active people. Make them an action plan, help them, and make the first presentations for them. Use the system. I would like to talk about this at another time," Markus said. "It is very important that you do not omit these categories of people, because by calling them, you make your business grow."

"Spend your time making presentations. The more presentations you make, the more you become good, and the more new customers and collaborators you find. Plan and make presentations for your team. Give the necessary support and become their mentor. Remember to be a good example. If you can do 5–7, or 10 appointments a day, your business partners will want to imitate you. If you do little but expect your team to do a lot, you won't succeed. People do what you do, not what you tell them to do. The third group of actions that bring earnings are the new contacts. When a person fails to generate new contacts in network marketing, he goes into crisis. He says after a while: 'I don't know who to call,'" Markus explained.

"I am very good at making new contacts. I'm not saying this to brag. I don't think it's my innate talent. I believe that this ability was acquired by necessity. When I started working in the marketing network, my people list wasn't very big. My family and my relatives were in Russia. My knowledge in Italy was limited to a group of friends, some acquaintances, and some work colleagues. I could not call my friends from childhood, school, or university. They were all too far away. So, I had to learn how to contact people. I made so many mistakes. But now I know the methods, and I am very effective in contacting people. In fact, I do training for people who want to learn this art, where I teach people to make good contacts everywhere," I said.

Markus complimented, "Brava! The ability to make new contacts is very important."

At that point, I knew I wanted to continue to develop this ability of mine, because it is one of the actions that brings greater profit.

Renew Your Commitment Regularly

"Sometimes you find people in your organization who complain that they can't sell products and can't find new business partners. People usually start with great enthusiasm. They start with great results and are great for the first 30, 60, and even 90 days. And then something happens around 90 days. For some mysterious reason, the person is no longer able to get the results from before. Some say that perhaps this person has become too lazy. But actually, he is doing the same actions he did before. Or someone says that the person has become too knowledgeable. But how do you make yourself too wise in just 90 days? Obviously, the cause is not that. I call it the 90-day phenomenon," Markus said. "In this period, it happens that the person has lost the initial enthusiasm. It can happen for various reasons. Maybe someone told him that the product doesn't work so well, or told him some negative network marketing stories, or gave him some wrong advice, which he continues to use. The results are starting to fall. Safety and enthusiasm also begin to diminish. It's a vicious circle," he explained.

"But how do you break this vicious circle?" I asked.

"First of all, when you feel this thing, stop and think. Surely, your beliefs disagree with what you are doing. Try to remember what happened. Maybe you failed to make a sale, and your safety has decreased. What else? Surely, you are convinced of something right now, but you are not convinced of the right thing. You don't have the same attitude that led you to success in the business. Determine what the weak point is in your beliefs: doubts about the product, company, business or service. Ask yourself how you felt when you were at the top of your professional performance. How did you talk? How did you move? What did you think about the product and the activity?

"Do everything to restore your attitude. Write down all the strengths of the product and its benefits. Write the strengths of the company and the marketing plan. Watch the videos that the company provides you. Go to an event, and talk to the successful people in your company. Events are a source of motivation, and I would like to talk to you about their importance. Do everything you can to get your motivation and your belief back on top!" Markus exclaimed.

"This phenomenon can happen even more often than 90 days. We are all surrounded by negative people, energetic vampires, and even by envious people. Always keep in mind your goal: to become independent and free from an economic point of view. Don't let yourself be deviated from anything or anyone. Always renew your motivation and conviction. I do this too," Markus said. "Sometimes even two or three times a week," he revealed.

If even a successful person like Markus always needed to renew his motivation, I decided to do it myself, regularly!

The 90-Day Plan

We met up with Markus and his assistant, in the lobby of a beautiful hotel, where Markus had been interviewing. I had already done my run along the beach, remembering Markus's advice to be in good shape, and I was wearing an elegant suit. Even Markus and his secretary were elegantly dressed.

"I see you've heard my advice," he smiled. "And now that you know the four qualities of a successful person, you know that you have to act massively, and you also know the actions you need to do. Your actions must bring you earnings. Become a master in inviting people, making presentations, and creating new contacts. Spend 80% of your time on this. The remaining 20%, you divide into planning and control. Learn to delegate all things that are not profitable. We are all very busy today. However, things like washing the car, fixing the house, even shopping and cooking, take away a lot of time and energy. Focus on the things that bring you profits, now that you also know the phenomenon of the 90 days. You know how to manage your motivation; try to keep it as high as possible, and do as many actions as possible.

"Think about the results you want to have after 90 days. How many new customers do you want to acquire? How many new collaborators? How many business partners would you like to help during this time? What new qualification or turnover do you want to reach?

Based on these goals, plan your time and your

business.

"It won't happen overnight, but you have to learn how to manage your time. A 90-day plan helps you keep pace and be productive. Write down all the things in your life that don't bring you money and that you can delegate. Think about the people you can ask for help. Do you have a partner at home? Do you have older children who can do some housework? Do you have a retired friend who would like to round up a little and can do office work? Do you have a neighbor who is good at managing Facebook pages? Delegate these things to them. Focus on the main activities that bring you profits. Now, sit down and start planning your 90 days, based on what I told you. Take an hour and let me see the result," Markus said.

I started creating my 90-day plan, based on the activities that bring in earnings.

In these years, I have made many of these plans. It was not easy, especially learning to delegate. But only by practicing can you become a master. I also help my collaborators, when they ask for it, to do targeted work plans that lead to results. I also do it with people who come to me for coaching sections. You too, dear reader, can create your 90-day plan. Take an hour and plan.

9

The Ultimate Secrets of Success

Our Business is the Business of People

We were sitting on Markus's terrace, talking about our business.

"Many people," said Markus, "believe that network marketing is a business of selling products, when in reality, it is the business of people. In most cases, people do not buy products because they are of good quality, although there are many high quality products on the market. People buy because these products have been proposed by us, and because we have explained to them the benefits they have, the problems they can solve, and above all, because we place ourselves well against them, and they trust us. They know that we offer them good assistance and we don't abandon them. For the same reasons, people become business partners. Of course, the company is very important; it is also that the marketing plan is generous, but if the person does not want to have anything to do with us, we have a problem. Surely, he will not want to become our business partner and, even if he becomes one, he will not work with us for long.

"Therefore, a good network marketing professional must learn to create and maintain relationships. You become a lovable, interesting, and fun person. Learn to listen even more than talk. Make people feel good in your company. Become their friend and adviser. You don't have to give advice unless they ask for it. However, meet the people who can be your potential customers, and stay in touch with current business partners, especially those more active. Try to create the relationship of friendship with everyone, and after each conversation, I suggest you write about what was talked about, the news, and recurrences. Keep in mind the birthdays and the important data of the people. They will always be very happy when they receive a greeting message or a phone call from you. Try to understand the problems of the people you know, and be a good friend. Create and maintain knowledge and friendships. Do it consistently," he concluded.

"Can you give me an example?" I asked.

"Yes, now I will show you how I do it," said Markus. "Be prepared for lunch with a friend," he added.

How To Create Quality Contacts

We got into the car and went to a beautiful restaurant. I was in a convertible, and along the way, I admired the palms. The hot wind blew through my hair and gently caressed my face. I felt completely happy. We arrived in front of a beautiful room. I looked at the cars that were parked: A Jaguar, a Rolls Royce, an Aston Martin, and other prestigious cars were parked in the parking lot in front of the restaurant. A man came to meet us, with a smile that seemed to contain all the happiness of the world, and once in front of us, he said, "Good morning, Mr. Markus; nice to see you. Your table is already ready."

"Very well, Rodrigo," Markus said, and we headed for the dining room. I looked around; it was beautiful. Large crystal chandeliers hung from the ceiling, and the white silk curtains protected us from the sun, giving the impression of freshness, cleanliness, and immensity to the place and to the tables. The room was full of elegant people who conversed in low voices, and among them, some sent nods of greeting to Marcus. It was clear that he was at home here.

"My friend is coming soon," said Markus. "In the meantime, I'll explain a few things to you," he added. "Many people ask me where I find quality contacts. I'm out of your circle, from your comfort zone, right? There are few people who were born rich, especially in network marketing, because it is an opportunity that allows simple and normal people to become wealthy, and sometimes very rich. But to find quality people who have the money, and who can afford high quality products and are also interested in new income, you have to get out of your circle of influence. And slowly, your circle of knowledge begins to change," he said.

"Yes," I confirmed. "I see that not all my friends or acquaintances can afford high quality products that our company sells. Maybe they still spend money on useless things, but among my friends, not many have become my clients. This is why I asked myself where I could get to know the people who are interested and can afford the high quality products."

"Right," said Markus. "If you want to become a successful person, you have to choose the best people who have the chance. You must become one of them. For this reason, don't spend too much time with old friends; start attending new places. Choose a more beautiful and prestigious place nearby that is within your reach, put on your best dress, and go to lunch there. Even if you only have one salad, you will begin to settle in, get to know each other, make new contacts, and develop new friendships. Don't always eat with the usual people you have known for a lifetime, who can't buy anything from you. Spend your time effectively. Go where you find quality people, and start interacting with them. Create contacts, friendships, and relationships, and they will then ask you what you do, and if you create a relationship of trust, they will become your customers or business partners."

"See," continued Markus. "Now, I'll see you with my client; he has been using our products for several months and is happy; and in recognition, sometimes I invite him to lunch. Thanks to him, I also acquired other clients: his friends. Without him, I would never have come to them."

As we conversed, a man arrived, dressed very well, with grizzled hair. He greeted us cordially, and shortly afterwards, we began lunch. We talked about our families and about events that would take place over the weekend in Miami, and I had a wonderful time.

Don't Abandon Your Base

I asked, "But when you told me that I no longer have to have lunch with my friends, do you mean that I really have to abandon them?"

Markus laughed, and then replied, "You must never abandon the people with whom you have a trusting relationship, who believe in you, and who know you well. It is your strong point. Maybe not all of them will want your products, or they will not believe in business, but this is their choice. I simply told you not to spend all your time with them, and to create new contacts, especially quality contacts. As Jim Rohn said, 'You are the average of the five people with whom you spend the most time.' Observe those with whom you spend most of your time, and you will become just like them. How much do your friends earn? What conversations do they make? What are the objectives? But anyway, stay in touch with the people you trust," he concluded.

Shortly thereafter, he resumed, "Every now and then, new business partners don't want to talk to people they know well, and they try to call strangers, or look for people on the Internet or on Facebook. This is a difficult path. And it's normal; you also don't easily trust an unknown person, do you?" he asked. "Would you rather do business with a friend, and buy more easily from a true friend?" he added.

"Yes, it's true," I confirmed.

"Precisely for this reason," he said, "keep in touch with your circle of knowledge. But don't forget to stay away from those who are always negative and critical. Even if sometimes it happens to you, don't argue with them. Keep these people away by not wasting your energy, and stay in touch with positive people. Even if they don't buy right away, always ask them if they know someone who could be interested," he advised me.

"Yes!" I exclaimed. "Nora taught me this. I took the references, right?"

"Absolutely," said Markus. "Very well, keep in touch with your best friends and acquaintances; meet with them for coffee, lunch, or a walk," he added. "Even if there are people you haven't heard from in a long time, it's never too late. Call them, send them a message, and try to arrange a meeting to reconstruct the report. Be interested in their lives, try to help them solve their problems, be useful in some way, and always ask them to introduce you to someone who might be a good acquaintance; and you will see that you will always be surrounded by friends, and your business will always grow," concluded Marcus.

Where To Find New Contacts

"I understand, Markus. I have to take good care of the relationships with the people I know, especially the positive people, and I also have to get out of my comfort zone to find quality people. But where can I find them?" I asked again.

"There are so many places. For example, we are in the wellness business; where can you meet people who are interested in wellness?" he asked.

"In a gym," I replied. "Or in a yoga class," I added.

"Perfect. By the way, are you a member of a gym? Do you remember that I told you that successful people have to be fit?" he asked.

"Yes, sure. Like James Bond," I said, making both of us smile.

"Yes, just like him," replied Markus.

"Yes, I'm enrolled in a gym," I then returned seriously, answering his question a few seconds before.

"Well. And do you go there regularly?" he asked.

"Yes, at least three times a week."

"Perfect. When you do exercises, try to be sociable. Look at people, greet them, make some jokes, and try to be nice. There are also many Pilates, yoga, aerobics, or Zumba courses. There are so many people interested in wellness. Start a conversation, get the phone numbers, and create a friendship. Invite the person to drink coffee. By creating friendships in this way, you will surely find the right people. What else could you do to find those that are interested?" he asked.

"I can look at Facebook to see if there are groups that are related to wellness," I suggested.

"Brava, that is a good idea. Try to get to know people on Facebook, but don't send them promotions, and don't sell them online. Nobody likes being pushed to make a purchase, especially from people we don't know well. Sending spam can damage your image, and even that of your company. And it's not effective at all," he suggested. "Try to get to know a person. First create a relationship of sympathy and friendship. Remember that our business is a business among people," he explained. "It doesn't matter what kind of product your company sells. Try to think about where your ideal client or business partner could be. People like to meet in groups for interests. And it is in these places that you will find the people who will be happy to be your customers and do business with you."

Attend Fairs and Events

"To find so many good contacts, you could also attend specific trade fairs that take care of your industry," suggested Markus. "For example, in your case, and based on the sector you work in, search the Internet for a wellness fair nearby. There are two ways to attend a trade show. You can participate as an official partner; you could then take a stand or a space alone, or even with some of your collaborators and colleagues. Of course, it is the most expensive method because you have to rent the space, spend a figure to put a banner, and in addition, you must have enough promotional material with you. But it is also the solution that brings so many possibilities to meet new people interested in the subject. Furthermore, having the space, you can talk quietly with people, and you could even make a presentation, a real sale, or a registration; and surely, having a stand in a fair also gives a more prestigious image," he said.

"Sometimes when you are a participant in a fair, they also allow you to be part of a seminar or a conference, where you can explain the advantages of your products, and make a presentation from the stage. In this case, you would reach many interested people, and you would appear with an expert," he added.

"You have to evaluate yourself, if you have enough money to deal with this option. A cheaper but equally effective method is to go to the fair as a visitor. It costs you an entrance ticket. Dress elegantly, show off your best smile, prepare many business cards, and meet many people. Talk to them, briefly explain what you do, and get their contacts. This is the most important thing," he stressed.

"Many people come to the fairs but end up having so many brochures and business cards that they no longer look because of lack of time. Instead, you pick up the contacts and, within 72 hours, contact these people, tell them that you met at the fair, ask them if they need some more information, and start creating a relationship with them," Markus continued, as he always had my full attention.

He paused and resumed, "There are also networks and events on the various issues, and it can also happen that they are free. They are usually organized by various associations or companies. Try to identify the most suitable for your business, choose some, and go visit them.

The golden rule here is to *listen more and talk less*. Socialize, get to know people, and ask for their business cards or contact information, and start to establish a conference-to-conferencefriendship/event-to-eventrelationship. Try to attend these events on a regular basis, and you will see that there are people who have potential. Make yourself known, and maintain the relationships you have created on these occasions. It's a longer process, but our business is a marathon and not a sprint.

Create Contacts Anywhere

Markus continued to teach me how to create new contacts, and he told me how to learn to recognize people with potential, especially if they were people who could have been our collaborators.

"Look for people who seem to be positive, with a nice smile, and who speak in a beautiful way. When you happen to be in a restaurant, shop, or anywhere else, notice how people act in different situations. If you notice that a person takes responsibility and wants to help other people, it is very likely that he is a suitable person for our business. Because our business repeats, it's a business of relationships between people," he said.

"The people I know, who have achieved success in our business, worry about the others. They want to make them feel good and try to solve their problems, and they take responsibility. This happened to me a little while ago. I had arrived at a hotel, where I had booked a room to hold a meeting with my closest collaborators, and when I arrived, hours before the event, it turned out that the room I had reserved, had been mistakenly booked by another person. The receptionist who was on duty was confused and began to apologize, without proposing a solution. He said he would let me talk to a superior.

"A young man came out of the office, who had not listened to the problem, and asked me to wait a few minutes, promising that he would remedy it in some way. He managed to contact a hotel, 200 meters ahead of ours. The price was the same, but to make up for the mistake his staff had made, he sent us a water tray and a tray of snacks for the coffee break," he said.

"I immediately saw that this boy had potential, because he was able to handle sudden situations, take responsibility, and be a leader. I told him that I was looking for people who could take responsibility for a new project, and I asked him for his contact number. After a few days, he became my collaborator. Within three months, he made his career.

"This means finding people with potential. Even when I go on a plane," Markus continued, "I always try to converse with the people who are next to me, or when I see a person who might be interested in the product or has the characteristics to become a collaborator. Subsequently, within the 72 hours, I will give a presentation if the journey is short; or if the journey is 10 or 12 hours, I will do the presentation immediately. The important thing is to develop the habit of creating contacts everywhere," concluded Markus.

10

Connect and Grow Rich

Network Marketing is a Mentoring Activity

"Many people think that network marketing is a sales activity, but this is not the case. Surely, you have to sell the products and share them with others, because without turnover, there are not even earnings; but the most important and stable results come when a person creates his team, and teaches people who started the business with him. And then these people do the same with their business partners. In network marketing, it is important to create duplication. This means that your people repeat your actions. Invite and present, and when they begin to teach their teams the same simple steps, start your passive gain. That's why I see network marketing more as a teaching job than a sales job," said Markus.

I followed his words carefully.

"It's like raising a child. As soon as he is born, he cannot do anything; then he learns to stand, walk, and talk. The same thing happens, in most cases, with our new team members. When a new business partner starts the business, he is enthusiastic about the product, and likes the company and the business; however, he does not yet know exactly what to do. It is our task to teach them to set goals, understand their *why*, create the contact list, and to make calls and make their first appointments. We must be with him or her, and even make the first presentations for him until he learns to do them alone and effectively. If we work with a webinar system, or call via Skype, we must support the person after the presentation. We must teach them to respond to objections, and to conclude meetings with a sale, an enrollment, the requesting of references, or making another appointment. Prepare yourself for patience, and teach your people to maintain a positive attitude, even in difficult times. Always be with them; motivate them and teach them everything you know," he suggested.

This is an important lesson I received from Markus. Today, when a person starts working with me, I try to teach them everything, step by step. And when I train people who want to learn network marketing, I always remind them that our business is a mentoring and teaching business.

The Code of Honor

"I developed this honor code a few years ago, when I was at the beginning of my network marketing career," said Markus. "I became good at selling products, presenting them, and finding new business partners. But despite all my efforts, people didn't stay in business for long, and this disturbed me. I realized that before starting to work with a person, we have to make a kind of pact that we both need to respect. And if this pact is not respected, I don't work with this person. They are the rules we are committed to follow," he explained.

"Tell me," I said. "I want to know too."

He went to his desk, took a sheet from the drawer, and gave it to me. On it was written the team's honor code.

The Team's Honor Code:

1. We care about our collaborator. The first meeting is within 48 hours of the start of the activity.
2. We work together as a team.
3. We share products with people to improve their lives.
4. We share the business with people to give them the chance to have more wealth in their lives.
5. We will only use real stories and real numbers.
6. We promise little, but we give much more.
7. Promote all your company's events, and participate in as many events as possible.
8. We are an example. We encourage others to be better.
9. We recognize integrity as our main value. We work in an ethical and honest way.
10. We have come here to win and dominate the market.

"Wow!" I exclaimed. "Fantastic! I really like it! Can I create an honor code of my own?" I asked.

"Of course! What would you like to add?" asked Markus.

"For example:
- Keep daily contact with your sponsor and team.
- Be on time for appointments.
- If you have problems or doubts, ask your up line (sponsor).
- Promote and build your sponsor.
- Always keep your motivation high.

- Learn something new for your business every day.
- Help all those who need your help.
- Only work with those who want to work with you."

"Plan and regularly monitor your actions," I said.

"Excellent," said Markus. "I see you have so many good ideas! The honor code can also be used in your family, with your children," he said. "But let's get back to our business. Now, sit here and write the honor code for your team. Write up to 10 rules to help you establish and maintain effective contact with your business partners. Do it now. Put the timer on 10 minutes, and create it," he suggested.

Do it too, dear reader; it will help you in business and in life.

Promote and Participate in Your Company's Events

"In our business, it is very important to be convinced of our business, our products, and the company. The motivation must always be high, and it is not an easy task. We are surrounded by negative information; we hear it everywhere: radio, TV, whoever surrounds us."

"One of the best methods I know of," said Markus, "to keep the motivation high, is to attend company events. They are essential for those who want to succeed in our business. Participate in as many events as you can, attend weekly meetings, if you are in your city, and invite guests. Attend regional and national events to meet the people who work in your country, and talk to the best and learn from the leaders. Also, take part in international conferences, because the real leaders are born of these events. I can't explain what happens in big events, but there's magic. During these events, people are transformed. They gain confidence and determination, and make the decision to do business in a serious manner. You have already attended the events, and you know how much energy and how many new things they bring.

"I met so many people during my career in this industry, and I have heard many very interesting stories. There were people who had recently started working in the company and were taking part in an event, and they took this activity seriously and professionally, and achieved surprising results. I also met people who had been in business for a while but didn't do much, and they didn't have much success. But they came to an event, and their results have changed. And they never stopped. They participated in other corporate events, brought their team with them, reached increasingly higher goals, and earned more and more. But it all started from a conference. Do everything to participate in events, and bring as many of your team as possible to these events. Talk to people, and let them understand the importance of events for their success. Get tickets for each event first; be an example. Make sure all your leaders go to the event and bring their teams with them. Explain to new business partners that without this step, it will not be possible to achieve great success. We must surround ourselves with positive people, from whom we can learn something. We must be where we can meet them, and if not at events, then where we have the chance to talk to them and learn from their experience. And then the events are very funny. We know new places and new people. The trips you will take with your team will give all participants lots of emotions and good memories for a lifetime," he explained.

There, on the Markus terrace, looking at the ocean, I

promised to go to every business event, and to bring as many people as possible with me. During these years, I have participated in every event that makes my company available or that we have organized with my colleagues. We owe much of our success to having respected this rule:

Promote your company's events, and participate in as many events as you can, with your team.

Follow the System or Create It

"To succeed in network marketing, and create a residual income or profit, it is necessary to follow the system. It should be simple to perform and repeat. This is necessary to make it possible for every person in your team, especially new people, to learn certain actions and teach others quickly. Let's take an example: When a new person starts working in network marketing, he must register, try the products, and meet his sponsor or mentor. He or she should train the beginner in the system. Teach them to set goals, to plan contacts, to qualify them, and to invite people. This is the first step. The company and the team should have a series of activities through which a person with basic skills can actually make presentations to find clients and new business partners. You already know that these may include a meeting, a Skype call with the sponsor or an up-line mentor, or a webinar or a business meeting in a hotel.

"Another option is to also watch a company video about the products or the business, with the guest, or have the presentation of the products and the company at a person's home, together with his friends or relatives (launch evening). It is important that a new person has different situations in which to invite his guests and, more importantly, after performing these simple actions, there is his sponsor or another expert on the team to help him answer questions from guests, to conclude the sale or register a new team member. How do you check if the system works? Every new person on your team should respond positively to the question: "Can I do it?"

"Everyone can invite a friend to a meeting, watch a short video with him, send a link to a webinar, then call his guest, and introduce him to his mentor. Gradually, the new person will learn how to make presentations and answer guests' questions. But first, it needs an exact algorithm—a system of what to do—in order to acquire the first customers and business partners. There is a system in our company and in our team, and it is very simple and effective. It is very important to learn how to use it and explain it to new team members, as well as make sure they will follow this system," he concluded.

If, dear reader, your company or team does not have this system, you can now create it yourself. Think and write, using the principles above, which system you can create, to work with it and offer it to new business partners. Write down all the steps, use it, and teach it to your team members; and your business will grow and prosper.

The Importance of Charity

"In our business, and indeed in life," continued Markus, "to be successful and happy, it is necessary to help others. And now, I'm not talking about our business partners and customers. Now I'm talking about helping those less fortunate than us. You have probably noticed that rich and famous people are very often engaged in charity. Some say they do it to pay less tax, or because they are ashamed to earn so much when there are so many poor people in the world. People who think this way simply don't understand the laws of the universe, and the successful people who know these laws, use them for their own good," he said.

"And what are these laws? Well, this is a long conversation," said Markus, "but now I'll tell you one of the most important laws: *to give more to receive, or return the good to the universe, to get what you want.* Since time immemorial, many world religions have said that charity is a good and necessary thing. This is evidenced by Christianity, Buddhism, Judaism, Islam, and other religions. And this is no accident. This is a great law: to give a part of what you receive to people in need. I advise you to allocate, from all the money you receive—in the form of salary, earnings in network marketing, a loan repaid suddenly, etc.—at least 10% to charity. Some say that when they become rich, they will start helping others. It does not work like this. First, start doing charity, and you will have the chance to become wealthy.

"The best network marketing companies have their charitable funds. Our company also has this beautiful tradition: we can donate money or send food to poor children or needy adults. This is a great undertaking, and I urge you to always give a part of your earnings to this charity, as well as any other that you might like," he suggested.

"In fact, when I met our company, I, as a mother, was very impressed by the fact that we have our own charitable foundation through which we can help children, who sometimes have nothing to eat. We can also help them get a better education and live a happy and dignified life," I said.

By giving money to charity, we give them the opportunity to improve their lives and the world as a whole. But by improving the lives of other people, we are improving our lives, because we are doing good and noble deeds, and the universe will surely reward us.

Every time I speak from the charity stage, I invite my listeners to not only think about its importance, but I call them to action.

Dear reader, stop and do something now. Visit the website of your favorite charity, and give your contribution. It is important to do this from the heart, and with a sincere desire to help. And you decide yourself to do it regularly; for example, once a month. And you will see how your life starts to change for the better.

Connect and Grow Rich

The time had come to greet Markus. I thanked him heartily for his valuable advice; we hoped for success and returned to Italy. I had learned a lot from my mentors, but I knew that the road ahead of me had just begun. I realized that a lot of work was waiting for me. I was looking forward to meeting new people, making calls, giving presentations, and having meetings, webinars, and events. Remembering the teachings of my teachers, I learned (and I do it constantly) to keep the motivation at a high level. I know how important it is to be convinced that your company's products, the company itself, its business plan, and your service are the best. I remember my business partners. I'm talking about the importance of being 100% sure and convinced of those who come to me for advice and attend my training courses.

Years of hard work, fantastic journeys, and development of one's abilities and talents have been very intense, and not always simple. I am very grateful to all those I met on this trip, and in particular to the founders of the company I work with, for the unique opportunity to change my life and the lives of thousands of other people for the better, and for their honesty and integrity, their hard work, and the recognition received. Thanks to my wonderful and loyal customers, and also those who have not yet used the products, as well as those who buy our products occasionally. I remember, with gratitude, the people who came to discover our opportunity and refused it, because they taught me to receive the "no" without despair, and gave me the opportunity to analyze my mistakes.

I am grateful to the people who started a business with me but for some reason left—we made a part of the journey together, we met as people, and sometimes we became friends. With many of these people, I continue to maintain good relationships, because friendship is a wonderful part of life and remains even when the collaboration ends. I am very grateful to the people who joined my team and started building a business with me, working shoulder to shoulder, day after day, month after month, and year after year. I appreciate and respect these people very much for their self-confidence, their dreams, and their desire to win. I firmly believe that these people, my friends, and my colleagues will reach their goal and realize their dreams. Thank you very much, my dear business partners!

Thank you, dear reader, for reading this book to the

end. I have tried to explain the principle of uniting people and changing their lives—and also yours—for the better; as well combining some simple skills that you can learn to succeed and be financially independent. I know that if you follow these principles step by step, perform the necessary actions actively and regularly, and you surround yourself with the right people, firmly believing in your project, company, and product, and above all, in yourself, you will succeed! If you need advice or have any questions, feel free to contact me. Leave your question or request on the website, www.connectandgrowrichbook.com.

Connect and grow rich! I wish you much success on this wonderful journey!

About the Author

Natalia Dikun was born in Russia, and successfully graduated from the Academy of Culture, in St. Petersburg, with a degree in Cultural Studies and Tourism Management. During her student years, she worked with prominent cultural and art representatives in St. Petersburg, and studied the basics of entrepreneurship. In 1995, Natalia went to work in Italy. She lived in the north of Italy and worked in the tourism business. Then she worked as an export manager for the Eastern European market, with various companies. Despite a good salary, she was looking for financial stability for herself and her family. She, alone, raised her son and wanted to have additional income, as well as the possibility to create residual income. Therefore, in 2013, at the invitation of a friend, she began to work with a large network marketing company. Natalia, being an ambitious and resolute person, always looked for an opportunity to improve her life. She attended courses from such famous trainers as T. Harv Ecker, Robert Kiyosaki, Brian Tracy, Jim Rohn, Anthony Robins, and others. Having started working in the network marketing industry, she applied the knowledge she gained. Being an energetic and goal-oriented person, and working hard and actively, Natalia made a rapid career. During the first one and a half years, she became one of the top leaders of the company she still works with. One of her priorities has always been the desire to help people. During her career in this industry, she has helped hundreds of people improve their quality of life and increase their income. Natalia helps with advice, counseling, and training, which are based on personal, successful experience and long years of practice. She gained extensive experience in working in network marketing, and outlined it in her first book.

Currently, Natalia lives in London, where she continues to be engaged in network marketing, and also gives consultations and conducts trainings. If you want to learn how to become financially independent from a simple employee, travel the world, and radically change your life for the better, this book is for you.

If you want to invite Natalia as a mentor, leave your request at www.connectandgrowrichbook.com, or write to: wealth@connectandgrowrichbook.com.

She will be glad to help you, and will spend the first hour of consultation for free.

If you want to hire her as a speaker for your event, or invite her as a guest for your radio or television show, please e-mail wealth@connectandgrowrichbook.com with your request.

If you want to buy more books, please visit: www.Amazon.com.

If this book has inspired you, then the best thing you can do is give it to your friends, and be an example to them. In network marketing, as in other businesses and other areas of activity around the world, people are needed who can set an example for everyone.

The author wishes you to be such a person!

www.ingramcontent.com/pod-product-compliance
Lightning Source LLC
Chambersburg PA
CBHW060904170526
45158CB00001B/497